Jogging From Memory

Rob Buckman

Jogging From Memory
OR
LETTERS TO SIGMUND FREUD VOL. II

Illustrations by Martin Honeysett

The Leisure Circle

This edition published 1981 by
The Leisure Circle Limited
York House, Empire Way, Wembley, Middlesex

Rob Buckman writes a regular column for
General Practitioner and some of the items in
this book first appeared there.

First published 1980

SBN 434 98000 5

Printed and bound in Great Britain by
Biddles Ltd, Guildford and King's Lynn

Contents

TO:
B.B.B. & I.F.B. and J.F.S. & J.E.S.
for showing me the way
(in several different directions)

ROGUE MAIL
My Cousin Rachel

Dear Doctor Freud,

I am fascinated by your idea that — if I understand your description of internecine psycho-social counter-dependence correctly — your family can drive you bonkers. For instance, your analysis of the Oedipal mother-son involvement sounds jolly interesting. Although not much fun, if you don't mind me saying so. But it does occur to me that you haven't given sufficient attention to other family relationships that, in my opinion, do cause certain people to undergo something that we transactional phenomenological psychoanalysts call 'blowing their stack'. I refer to cousins. Of course I realise that cousins aren't quite as important as mums and dads, or parents as you call them, but although one cousin does less damage per kilogram body weight than a closer relative, when they occur in large numbers they can cause considerable problems. Like locusts. Or plague germs. Perhaps a case illustration might help me convince you of my thesis.

Personally, I have thousands of cousins. I have more cousins than anyone I know — excluding my cousins, who seem to have even more cousins than I have. I have cousins in Canada, California, Australia, South Africa, Wembley, New Zealand, Hull, New York, Switzerland, Manchester and Cannes. I have a whole clutch of them in Israel, and every eleven years one of them arrives on our doorstep and says, 'Chow are you? Chi am Ullya and chi am very exciting to be chere.' Many of my cousins are involved in the arts — as directors, writers, producers, embezzlers and bouncers. A few are doctors, several are lawyers and a handful are a real handful. But none, dear Doctor Freud, are more so than Rachel.

My cousin Rachel lives in Canada at a pace so frenetic that it makes even David Frost look like a three-toed sloth with a sluggish thyroid. Mind you, that isn't as difficult as it sounds since, according

1

to a recent Gallup poll, 71 per cent of North Americans think that David Frost looks like a three-toed sloth with a sluggish thyroid, even without being compared to my cousin Rachel. Anyway, Rachel emigrated to Canada at the age of six, two days after being beaten by me at Chinese checkers, although she says the two events are not connected. In Canada Rachel now works as a senior journalist on a very famous magazine, and as a TV presenter on the major peak-time news programme. Her name over there is as famous as Alan Whicker's is over here, but, unlike Alan Whicker, she has been voted Canada's Most Beautiful Woman. It's not difficult to see why. She has what they call 'a striking figure'. Quite a few people get struck by it, especially if she turns round without warning. She has an enormous amount of *pzazz*, and what she lacks in *pzazz* she makes up for in *oomph*, *bewhoopah*, *kapow* and *chutzpah*.

Rachel — and I wonder what effect you think this has on the rest of the family, Doctor Freud — is an enormous success at everything she does. She and her husband wrote a novel about a political murder. The novel won the Edgar Allan Poe Award for crime-writing, the Spiro Agnew Trophy for political sensitivity, the John Wayne Shield for human values and the Nobel Prize for protein chemistry and domestic science (cakes division). Mind you, I should point out that our family has always been success-orientated. It has been a custom for generations among us that any member of the family who fails in a project or venture has to commit what the Japanese call *ha-haija-horokonu*, the ancient and traditional ceremony of asking the bank manager for a loan. One who does so is thereafter forbidden from holding his head high in the company of his fellow men for the rest of the afternoon.

Being so success-orientated and failure-intensive, our family has been compared to the Mafia — only without the violence, crime, Italian accents, pasta, slow-motion massacres or beautiful photography. Actually the comparison isn't quite as flaccid as it first seems, since our family has been very important in many major historical events. It's a sad fact that the name of our family has been deliberately excluded from the annals of history, despite the part it has played on both sides of the Atlantic (Butch Cassidy and the Buckman Kid), in science (Banting, Best and Buckman), and entertainment (Gilbert,

Sullivan and Buckman). As a family we have weathered this kind of cold-shouldering with the stoical, philosophical humility for which we are justly famous (St. Buckman of Assisi). With the exception of cousin Rachel.

Rachel has come over here to set the record straight, to delve into the family's early years and to re-establish its central role on the stage of history. Or something like that. Anyway, Rachel has been traipsing round the entire clan, dutifully recording everybody's childhood memories and background details. As I understand it she is trying to do a sort of North London version of *Roots*, with slight overtones of *Exodus* and *The Ten Commandments* plus the dramatic bathos of *Crossroads*. As she has reconstructed the history of our tribe, it seems that my dad will emerge as the Kunta Kinte of the Mile End Road. Apparently the Abraham Lincoln figure was Aneuran Bevan, and the Mississippi will be played by the Round Pond, Kensington.

This delving into the family background has, interestingly enough, bred a great deal of distrust. Despite Rachel's piercing intellect and brilliant insights (or possibly because of them), all those of our family who are having their Roots dug have responded rather warily. I suppose everyone has seen too many documentaries of the 'I-only-ask-the-question' type. You know the sort of thing: they begin with something like 'London's East End — teeming with a proud and dignified people; an enigma of history, these men are of the highest principles and deepest faith . . .' and end with ' . . . or are they?' I guess nobody really wants to be an enigma of history — it's so bad for business. So as Rachel probes around with her intellectual dentist's outfit, she has been copping a great deal of flak. Flak, I might add, of the highest psycho-social order — Oedipal, Clytaemnestral, internecine — the whole menu, even penis-envy. Except from me, that is. I actually volunteered to provide endless personal details of *my* past and origins, but Rachel wasn't interested. Apparently Canada isn't ready for a remake of *Bambi* yet.

Now the only reason I mention this whole business about families and cousins is simply that Rachel has just had to dash back to Canada at short notice. She has to complete a thirteen-part TV series on the health services and a six-part magazine series on immigration; she also has to negotiate her next novel and film, and have her perforating duodenal ulcer undersewn. So there's a bit of a gap in the project as far as our family is concerned. Well I just happened to mention that to a few of the boys in the Psychiatry Out-Patients Department, and they happened to let slip that the Freud family are a pretty fascinating bunch too. So what I'm wondering is whether your lot would like to step in (I admit it's at short notice) and feature in this 'great new novel-shortly-to-be-a-major-film-starring-Eli-Wallach'. I do hope that you and Mrs Freud — or rather both the Mrs Freuds, your mother and your wife — will be interested in the idea, and I enclose a stamped addressed envelope for your reply. Only do let me know soon. You see we've managed to get Marlon Brando to play Lord Lew Grade and he can only fit us in Thursday lunchtime.

Kindest regards to you and all the boys in Vienna,

ROB BUCKMAN

It's Enough to Make
the Blood Boil

You know me: always eager to save the National Health Service at any cost. Or at least always eager to save it any cost. Either way, I think I may have stumbled across a cost-saving idea which may well be hailed by administrators in the future as having all the ease and clean simplicity of the Battle of Stalingrad. In the course of this piece, by the way, for those of you who like quizzes there will be occasional quiz questions, so do stay awake; and for those of you who don't, there won't, so don't.

Now then, just as the famous chemist Friedrich Kekulé first thought of the ring structure of the benzene molecule while dozing in front of a fire (First quiz question: did he? Answer: yes he did. Score: two points for a correct answer.) so my idea came to me while I was working in the casualty department at St. Nissen's. And it is here that any resemblance between my story and that of Kekulé comes to an end; for unlike that famous German professor (1829-96), I was on night-shift. And not famous. Or even German. But, by complete coincidence, it was nearly half-past six (1829 on my digital watch) when a seriously injured man was brought into the department.

I must tell you straight away that this story has a happy ending and that the man made a perfect recovery, so don't start getting all edgy and panicky about it. At the time however, I spotted at once that the man was suffering from a condition known to us boys in the casualty racket as 'bleeding'. Those of you who have watched *General Hospital* might know the condition as 'massive haemorrhage', but not all of us doctors had televisions in those days. I was able to make this brilliant diagnosis by virtue of my incredibly thorough training. Our tutors at St. Nissen's had taken us over every aspect of emergency care in intricate and perfect detail, and I shall never forget the firm clinical grounding they gave us on bleeding. It went like this — Observa-

5

"NOT TONIGHT, I'VE GOT A HEADACHE"

tions: (a) the patient is white (b) the floor is red; Conclusion: bleeding. (Of course there may be the occasional snag with this approach. In some hospitals the floor may have been red all the time, and this can lead you astray; but in that event a brief phone call to the Hospital Secretary should put you right on this point.)

Having thus made the astute observation on my patient, I then proceeded to carry out the first step laid down in our casualty officers' manual: that is, I panicked. Having done that, I then set up a drip in each arm (of the patient), took some blood to find out his blood group for transfusion, gave him some plasma to be getting on with, applied pressure dressings to the wounds, did a cut-down to the vein in the left ankle, rang the X-ray department, put the operating theatres on stand-by and rang the duty surgeon. By now the scene was definitely beginning to resemble one of the earlier episodes of *General Hospital* (when they could afford larger casts). The technician from the haematology department (where they do all those clever cross-matching tests to make sure the patients get the right blood group given to them) brought in the first packets of cross-matched blood and I got three nurses to stand, each in charge of a drip, squeezing the plastic bags of blood to make them go in faster. This is called 'pressure transfusion' because nurses will only do it under pressure.

Now this is where I shall get a little technical and give you the second quiz question (or, if you didn't notice the first, the first). It is this: do you know where blood comes from? If your answer is 'No, I don't know where blood comes from' then you are probably COR-RECT, so give yourself three points and apply for a job as a doctor. If on the other hand, you *do* know where blood comes from, let me tell you you are probably INCORRECT, so give yourself five points and apply for a job as a Hospital Administrator. The answer is that blood comes from a fridge in the haematology department. For those of you who want to know more, and may be interested in a career in haematology, before the blood gets into that fridge, it comes from a little blue van labelled 'National Transfusion Service'. There's not many people know that. Anyway, the upshot of the whole thing is that blood *au nature* in the casualty department is very cold, and if you transfuse six pints of the stuff into a young chap very quickly you are in effect installing a sort of air-conditioning from the inside. For that reason (do stop me if I'm going too fast) we have these things called 'blood-warmers', which are long coils of plastic tubing that sit in a warm bath at 37°C and take the chill out of the stuff as it passes through — so it doesn't turn the poor recipient into a five-litre cross-matched ice-lolly.

Well then, while everybody was doing their 'General Hospital' bit and pressure transfusing away like billy-o, I nipped out and got the next three pints of blood from the haematology fridge, tossed them to one of the nurses and said, 'Righty-ho,' (I was young and hearty in those days) 'let's get this lot warmed up.' I then carried on being terrifically busy with the X-rays and the anaesthetist and so on. A few minutes later I turned back to the patient and found that the nurse and the three pints of blood had disappeared. To my horror, I then noticed that the three blood-warmers were standing idle in the corner of the room, and realised at once that whatever the nurse was doing with the blood, she wasn't putting it through the warmers as she was meant to.

All sorts of silly ideas go through your brain at times like this. I thought maybe the girl had nipped out to try and flog the stuff on the black market; maybe her boyfriend was a vampire, or even a barman with a novel line in cross-matched Bloody Marys. In increasing perplexity I wandered through the casualty department looking for her. She wasn't in the store-room, she wasn't in the sluice (where by some freak chance there happened to be the only phone extension in the hospital on which it was possible to dial direct to Australia), and she wasn't in the coffee room. I eventually found her in the kitchen. She had snipped the corners off the packets and was stirring the blood in a large saucepan on the stove. As I arrived, she was testing the temperature of the stuff with her elbow (presumably because she thought that her fingers were too dirty for the job). I stared aghast at her and then looked into the saucepan: what we had was nothing more than a three-pint Group A Rhesus-negative black pudding.

Being a man of considerable resource, I did the only thing possible in the circumstances. I snatched the saucepan from the wretched girl, rushed back to the patient and shoved the whole mess onto his chest like a poultice. Now the point of the story is that from the moment the ex-transfusion landed on his chest, the patient did terrifically well (though he later told me he had been unable to look a black pudding in the eye since, and was twice cautioned by the Commission for Racial Equality as a result).

It is therefore obvious to me that all those complicated cross-matching and grouping tests that they do in the haematology department are a complete waste of time. It is clearly a plot by haematologists to make themselves seem more important than they are. So what I say is, don't you go worrying your head about all those groups and transfusion-reactions and so on; you just go and warm the stuff up to about Regulo 7 and slap it on the patients' chests, and they'll do fine. If they're having brain surgery, then slap it on the back of their necks; if it's abdominal surgery, rub it on their tummies; and if it's gynaecology, well you'll think of something.

In fact we might even be able to organise something on an out-patient basis. We could set up a great big 20-litre cauldron of bubbling warm blood in the clinic and anybody who was a bit anaemic could come and dabble their fingers in it. It could mean the birth of a brand new speciality: 'Homeopathic Haematology' or 'Faith Transfusing'.

Well, there you have the outline of my plan to reduce costs in the Health Service. You must admit it's simple. But then of course, so was the British Leyland re-organisation plan, and look what *that* did for transfusion demands.

Apocalypse Later

The scene is a well-known television studio set up for our favourite up-to-the-minute arts programme. The presenter, hunched over his desk and wearing a tidy modern velvet suit and matching smile, is young BELVID DRAG. BELVID has a well-developed air of cool and sophistication, a very well-developed line of intellectual critique, and an exceptionally well-developed set of adenoids. It is this — or rather, it is these — that gives (or maybe give) him the somewhat nasal speech which has become the badge of his success. So popular is his voice now that several young trendies who had their adenoids removed in childhood have been seen dashing up and down Harley Street pleading for adenoid transplants. For some reason there has been a curious lack of donors. However, this is all by the by, for while we have been describing BELVID and dilating on his para-nasal lymphoid tissue, the titles of the programme have finished and BELVID addresses his fans.

BELVID: Haddo. Later in the prograb we'll be talking to Dadiel Baredboib about his dew recordig of Gershwid's orchestral arragemedt of the popular sog 'Shide Od Harvest Bood'. But first we look at the latest in a series of filbs about the Vietnab war. *(For the benefit of those readers who may be slightly hard of reading, we shall continue this reportage as if BELVID were speaking English.)* In the wake of such important and socially-conscious films as *Coming Home, The Deer Hunter* and *Apocalypse Now* comes the new potential block-buster, *Sweetness and Light.* It is as savage and as violently disturbing as its predecessors, and is directed by Francesco Maria Eisenmenger — a youngish director who received astonishing critical acclaim and enormous financial success for his searing and semi-documentary film about homosexuality in the American Mafia, *The Fairy Godmother.* His new film *Sweetness and Light* was shot on location in Borneo and has so far cost an astonishing twelve million dollars. It tells the story of a group of soldiers drafted into a Supply Platoon near the Haiphong Delta just after the Tet offensive. Their job is to deliver a relief supply of saccharine tablets and torch batteries (the sweetness and light of the title) to a beleaguered garrison run by an insane, sadistic colonel, portrayed in the film by Liza Minelli. On their journey the soldiers run out of emergency supply order-forms and are captured by representatives of a large North Vietnamese department store. They are interrogated by an equally sadistic insane Viet Cong colonel, played with extraordinary virulence by Glen Campbell, and are then taken to the department store where they are forced to play Russian roulette by the store detectives in the furniture department. The effect that this has on the young rookies leads the film to its inevitable, tragic, explosive, poignant and incredibly expensive ending. Earlier this week, I went to see Francesco Maria Eisenmenger at his luxurious Californian home, and I asked him first whether his family background had helped him deal with the complex moral issues involved.

We cut to a piece of film shot by the side of EISENMENGER'S massive swimming-pool. The first thing we see is the back of BELVID'S intellectual and deeply thoughtful neck. Beyond that we see EISENMENGER, hunched over, wearing a leather bomber-jacket and dark sunglasses. He is intense, hesitant, conscience-stricken and yet, at the same time, very wealthy. He appears to be thinking hard about what he is going to say. He also appears to be smoking a cigarette that has no printing on it.

BELVID: Has your family background helped you deal with the complex moral issues involved in this film?

EISENMENGER: Oh, I think so. Yuh. My mother was a Sicilian Catholic and my father was a Jewish transvestite and I . . . er . . . think that gave me a unique combination of Permanent Guilt and Original Sin. With uh . . . uh heavy sexual overtones.

BELVID: How do you view American guilt about the Vietnam war?

EISENMENGER: I think American guilt about the Vietnam war is like . . . uh . . . I guess . . . *(he looks vaguely about him)* . . . I guess it's like the water in my swimming-pool.

BELVID: It gets up your nose, you mean?

EISENMENGER: No, I mean that it starts out fine and clean until people start pissing in it. And you know, that's what makes your eyes sting — it's not the chlorine or nothing, they've done tests that show that, you know. I think that's what happens to everything in America — above the water-line everybody seems to be laughing and clapping their hands and having a ball and that, and all the time, below the water-line, they're killing the fish and causing all kinds of eye damage. That's how I see the . . . uh . . . American predicament right now, and that's why I always wear goggles when I go out.

BELVID: You had many problems during the shooting of *Sweetness and Light*, didn't you?

EISENMENGER: Yes we had.

BELVID: Were those problems simply due to the scale of the production?

EISENMENGER: I think maybe. Overall we had eight transport battalions, four hundred ten-ton trucks and half-tracks, six C5-Galaxies, two hundred F1-11s, and five Marine platoons with their big choppers.

BELVID: Gosh.

EISENMENGER: All in, we had maybe 250,000 extras to play the American army.

BELVID: Where did they all come from?

EISENMENGER: Iowa. We . . . uh . . . hired Iowa for the filming and shipped them all out to Borneo. You know Borneo looks a lot like Vietnam. Leastwise, it does now.

BELVID: There were terrible stories about the filming — it was said that hundreds of the actors and extras were very unhappy . . .

EISENMENGER: Yuh. . . .

BELVID: . . . and that many of them paid you in gold for the privilege of setting sail in flimsy boats back to Iowa; and that many of them sank or arrived in a pitiful state.

EISENMENGER: I think there are a great deal of human stories in any war . . . picture.

BELVID: Did any of them — as was alleged — actually play Russian roulette on the set, causing several deaths?

EISENMENGER: Russian roulette? Uh . . . I guess not. I know that on the North East corner of the set they . . . uh . . . had a lot of . . . uh . . . Russian salad. But roulette, no. Some of them played Russian whist — like Russian roulette only using marshmallow instead of bullets and a pillowcase instead of a gun. It's safer. And takes longer. And I guess it's very dull. Yuh. (*Long pause.*)

BELVID: I see. After *The Deer Hunter* and *Apocalypse Now,* don't you think everybody is getting fed up with the Vietnam war?

EISENMENGER: I hope not. I hope not. I hope not. Yuh, I . . . uh . . . hope not.

BELVID: You hope not.

EISENMENGER: I . . . uh . . . hope not.

We return to the studio and BELVID back at his desk.

BELVID: Francesco Maria Eisenmenger, there — christened by iconoclastic Hollywood as the one film director even gynaecologists look up to. Well, we're going to take a short break there — join us in a few minutes.

We see the commercial break starting. We wonder whether to join him in a few minutes. We think that, on balance, we probably won't. We think that we'll probably polish the spoons instead.

Language: A Doctor Speaks

Surprisingly, I was recently invited to become the Founder President of the Enfield and Harringay Philological Society. Wrongly assuming that philology was the posh word for wife-swapping, I accepted. The night before the inaugural meeting, the secretary-elect told me that philology was all to do with, as he put it, 'language and stuff like that'. I hurriedly re-wrote my presidential inaugural address and hereby append the speech as delivered, for your further edification and education. And stuff like that.

Ladies and gentlemen, I feel greatly honoured to be invited to give this address, and not only honoured but somewhat awed. For is not language one of the most important aspects of human behaviour? I think it's terrifically useful for communicating with, and, in line with current behavioural socio-dynamic psychologist theory, I would say that talking wouldn't be the same without it. Language is, when you come down to it, a whole . . . I mean it's a whole . . . language, isn't it? And much better at getting things over to other people than . . . than . . . well, you know.

However, I have chosen as the subject of my inaugural address not a song of praise to the goddess of language, but more a note of caution on the abuses and depredations currently being heaped on her altar. If the goddess Language is truly the White Cliffs of human expression, then she is being sadly eroded at the bottom. I have decided tonight to select a few of the more current abuses and misuses of language, the ones that I think are a bit more commoner and therefore dangerouser, and illustrate them for you. For these purposes I shall ignore the older errors, those that generations of grammarians have regarded as their *bêtes noirs* (a French phrase meaning literally 'black bets', *i.e.* money down the drain). I shall not be rehashing those schoolmasterish sentences such as 'Where did you get that book you know I don't like to be read to out of down from?' *(Laughter.)* I do not particularly object to ending a sentence with a preposition, but prefer, like most politicians and prostitutes, to end *my* sentence with a proposition! (*No laughter.*)

The first aspect of current abuse that I should like to illustrate is the common practice of converting nouns into verbs at random and without regard to grammar or propriety. For the purposes of this talk, I shall define as a noun any word pertaining to an object or abstract concept that has specific ontological significance within any given substantive contextual cognitive pattern. And of course a verb is a 'doing word'. Now the practice of converting a noun into a verb is long-standing. For centuries we have penned letters, pencilled drawings, and (more recently) telephoned our friends. But the practice of random and willy nilly conversion of *any* noun into a verb — one might say 'of verbing a noun' except one wouldn't be caught dead doing so (*no laughter*) — reached its apogee (or possibly apogeed) in an American movie when an unruly and ungrammatical youth said to his moll, 'Cigarette me, baby.' The mannerism caught on. Soon Americans were saying to each other, 'Let me lunch you.' The connotations were numerous. One could let oneself be *coffeed* early in the morning; the working-class continually *meat-and-two-vegged* one another while the aristocrats *Devonshire-clotted-cream-teaed* themselves; and the middle class executive, ever in a rush, simply *hamburgered* himself. After you have been *lunched* (or even lynched) the bill is checked and *credit-carded*, and if you don't want to keep the receipt you can always *dustbin* it.

I am sure you get the idea. It surprises me that the Americans — having had so much trouble with Messrs. Nixon, Ford and Carter — do not say things like 'the best man lost the ring, so the whole ceremony was completely *presidented*.' And from this inauspicious beginning, whither? Will the doctors of this country start doing it? Will patients soon be hearing things like 'Well, Mr Smith, I'm sorry to say that you have been *heart-attacked*.' Let us hope not. (Even if he has.) Will the practice then extend to abbreviations? Shall it be *de rigeur* (literally 'boring you stiff') to utter phrases like 'my new play was *BBCed* yesterday', 'I wrote a letter and *GPOed* it', or 'the Russian veto was *UNOed* this morning.' And if you fancy getting away from it all, you can always *P&O* off.

15

There is another trend coming to us on the wind of change blowing across the Atlantic — most of it small change unfortunately — and that is the tendency to append the suffix -*ise* to abstract nouns. Thus a citizen may announce that his house 'has been burglar*ised*'. This is indeed a crime of superfluity (by both parties) since we have totally acceptable alternatives freely available in 'a burglary has taken place', or even more simply 'the house was burgled'. This error carries with it an air of precision and technical knowledge which makes it attractive to the uninitiated. I fear that we will have, on the crest of the real crime wave, a second phraseological crime wave. Innocent passersby will soon be robbery-with-violenc*ised*, urban streets will be loitered-with-intent*ised* in, and rich merchants will be mugger*ised* or else abduction*ised* and grievously-bodily-harm*ised*, robber*ised*, assaul-t*ised* and, for all I know, sodom*ised* and simonized. The mere thought of all this dastardliness is enough to make me heart-failur*ised*. As we parliamentarians so often say, 'The -*ise* have it!' (*Absolutely no laughter at all.*)

Then there is the problem of the second remove. This is not another name for the debate on the abolition of public schools, but merely a way of suggesting that people are tending to forget where their words come from. A Vienna is a sausage designed or built in Vienna. A Hamburger is a flat cake of stuff dittoed (forgive me) in Hamburg. But there is no such city as Beefburg. Nor is there — even in Arizona — a town called SuperEggBrunchBurg; though there is still time for an oil magnate to build one. Nor does anyone live in TripleBeefyHawaiianBendyMaxiBurg, though many of us feel that we do. In the same vein, there is a well-known confection made with cherries and chocolate sponge called a Black Forest cake. If one invents a lemon-flavoured version of the cake, would it become Yellow Forest cake? Let us hope not. With the present standard of etymological orthodoxy, it would soon become Yellow River cake or even the highly xenophobic Yellow Peril cake. Even if it could be ediblised.

The final aspect of linguistic abuse that I would like to highlight under the precise glare of my philological scalpel is that of the chimaera. The uneasy alliance of verb and preposition in an ongoing and upcoming scenario. We may soon look forward to train passengers becoming involved in an offgetting situation, athletes starting an uplimbering run, students becoming outdropped (which sounds a little surgical), and of course prunes becoming — as everyone knows — throughgoing. Need I say more?

Well, ladies and gentlemen, this address has been little more than a preliminary survey of the field, an upwarming attempt on my part. If it has been too long or inaccurate, I do apologise in a downclimbing fashion; I just hope I haven't boredomised you. (*No laughter but a round of ecstatic shuffling of feet and a spontaneous burst of going across the road to the pub and stuff like that*.)

Waterside Up

I was on a radio programme recently when the conversation got round to Dylan Thomas. I thought they were talking about the rugger player, and I said I thought he used to be quite fast but was basically a bit of a fat oaf. Everyone was very impressed with my ascerbic wit and caustic criticism and suggested that I put together a collection of literary reviews and critical appreciation. I immediately agreed and then realised that I had never written any, so I thought I may as well have a crack at it now. Here then, is an extract from my forthcoming literary collection, provisionally titled 'The Moving Finger'.

I must admit that I approached the latest novel by W.D. Pillsworth with considerable trepidation. It occurred to me that in the last few years there have been a great many so-called 'nature novels' in which the author follows the adventures of a group of animals, expressing their thoughts and emotions in human language. At first glance even the idea behind Pillsworth's novel seemed rather uninspiring. In this book, called *Waterside Up*, Pillsworth has created a saga around the lives of a small family of North Sea haddock. Even at the outset, it might seem to a casual reader that any writer trying to express, in English, the thoughts of a haddock is going to encounter considerable difficulty, since haddock are not known to be particularly strong thinkers. And yet as the book progresses, we see that Pillsworth has coped with that problem almost by ignoring it. Large sections of the book are taken up with the atmospheric and naturalistic conversations between members of the family, giving a unique insight into what it actually means to be a haddock in the late twentieth century in the middle of the North Sea. ('It is salty, isn't it?' 'Yes it is.' 'It is wet, isn't it?' 'I'll say it is.' And so on.). Yet even at this level, the novel can be read as a stunningly simple, although barbed, comment on the human situation — as seen from sea-level.

But *Waterside Up* is much more than that, and gradually unfolds as a truly classical saga. Its hero is the middle brother of a family of eighty-seven haddock children whose name is Four-Eyes. At the beginning of the book he is emotionally neutral, uninvolved in his environment, regarding the North Sea simply as his omnipresent and unvarying nursery, restaurant, lavatory and bedroom (or, as we later find, brothel). His closest friend is a younger haddock called, because of his peculiar colouring, Floor-Polish. Floor-Polish is something of an heretic and keeps having ideas that are regarded by the rest of the tribe as obscene or taboo — for instance, he has a curious desire to know what chips taste like.

Together, Four-Eyes and Floor-Polish, joined by Floor-Polish's ugly sister Paper-Bag, go to visit one of the elders of the tribe, a so-called 'Toothless One' (this is a slight slip-up by Pillsworth, since haddock only lose their teeth when they lose their heads). This elder and sage, a fish of many summers called Eighty-Pee-a-Pound, tells the young ones of the history of the haddock race and of the Early Days when the haddock ruled the world. In those times there was no crime and no envy, only peace and plenty and very larger numbers of children. It seems that as a master race, haddock were kind and considerate both to other creatures and to the environment, their central dictum being expressed in the simple motto 'the sea is all around us'. Things might have continued in this pleasant fashion forever had it not been for a jealous and stupid member of the haddock royal family called Prince Fathead. Prince Fathead was apparently not only jealous and stupid but also weak and greedy and, in a desperate bid for personal power and short-term gain, he swam to Hull and signed a contract with a firm of trawlermen. As a result, the entire royal family of haddock went to visit the best hotels in the world but never actually came back. The rest of the haddock world, now leaderless and lacking a clear policy on any of the major issues of the times, became little more than a slave nation, indistinguishable from most other species of round white fish.

However, adds Eighty-Pee-a-Pound, it is widely believed among haddock all over the world that there is still a sort of earthly paradise or heaven, where old and good haddock go to be fed and looked after in tranquility and calm. This fishly Valhalla is called, in the language of the haddock, 'Lasvegas', and many of the older fish believe that it is not merely a legend but is a reality and is situated somewhere in the Atlantic Ocean. It is an idea that causes Eighty-Pee-a-Pound much difficulty as he tries to communicate it to his eager young listeners. This is because, in haddock speech, any bit of water they are swimming in at the time is called by the generic term 'the Sea', and any bit they are not occupying at that moment is known as 'more Sea'. Hence their sense of global geography is extremely limited, and their ability to talk about it almost nil.

Even so, these ideas ferment in the mind of young Four-Eyes and he discusses them frequently with his chosen mate Willow-hips and his mother Tugboat Annie. A few weeks later their part of 'the Sea' becomes heavily polluted by a new sewage effluent outlet — itself a poignant comment on Man as seen from the haddock viewpoint — and suddenly Four-Eyes has the idea of taking his family and friends to look for new and safe grounds in Lasvegas. If you have not read *Waterside Up* the bare story might seem to you rather dull, perhaps as a sort of haddock version of Gabriel Garcia Marquez' *One Hundred Years Of Solitude* and nothing more. If I have given that impression, I have done the book an injustice. For although any cheap novel-writer might have thought of the idea of a family of haddock emigrating from the North Sea to the Atlantic, it takes a genius of Pillsworth's calibre to have them make the journey overland.

In the major section of this picaresque fable, the family come ashore at Skegness — widely held to be one of the more picaresque parts of Lincolnshire — and then they turn towards the north. In considerable desperation, they pass through the outskirts of Sheffield, where they are forced to beg from door to door, and then, instead of heading towards Blackpool and 'more Sea', they make a mistake (due to inadequate road signs) and head towards the Lake District. It is in describing the isolated beauty and romantic wilderness of the lakes and fells around Derwent and Keswick that Pillsworth reaches the heights of his writing ability. His brilliant and vivid word-portraits of the rolling heather-clad hills and glassy lakes, almost unpopulated apart from the occasional rabbit or curlew (and, of course, the haddock), represent the very best of modern literature.

From the natural and unspoiled scenery of the Lakes, the haddock move on to the town of Carlisle where they have many adventures, including being short-changed by a rascally electrician. It is in Carlisle that a major row develops among the party, revealing a tragic and hypocritical flaw in the character of Floor-Polish who leaves them and sets up as a travel agent. Embittered but by no means disil-

"IS HE STILL BOASTING ABOUT THE SIZE OF THE HADDOCK HE CAUGHT SPEEDING YESTERDAY?"

lusioned, the rest of them carry on and eventually see the new 'more Sea' from a dockside at Solway Firth. It would be churlish of me to reveal the final ending of the book, except to add that I am sure there are overt religious overtones in the way they see what they believe is the one and only Lasvegas, and are then crushed to death by a falling crate of Swedish sexual aids.

As a novel, *Waterside Up*, although long, is a curiously subtle mixture of delicate fable, pointed allegory and inaccurate zoology. Yet it is strangely humourless. The one light touch is in the character of a callow yearling known as Hucklefin Berry — and even he is allowed only one joke. As if in tragic counterpoint, Berry points out another group of emigrating fish, says 'There's no home like plaice', and is immediately struck dead by what the haddock call in their own language 'a virus infection'. From that moment on, *Waterside Up* is no laughing matter.

Perhaps it is in the created language of the haddock that W.D. Pillsworth has made his greatest contribution to memorable fiction. In the same way in which Tolkein fans took to speaking Elvish, so, perhaps, the haddock tongue will gain currency. Particularly memorable is the verb 'to boffle', meaning 'to swim in water so polluted with untreated sewage that it is difficult to see very far in front of you'; a feeling familiar to many of us in the National Health Service. Also, I liked 'a praddler', meaning 'a young fish — usually a child — who is continually boffling while pretending he isn't.' Finally the haddock have a word for the most dreaded thing of all, the act of being hauled onto land by a hook, slit open with a sharp knife and boiled in oil: they call it 'being kissingered'.

I wish Mr Pillsworth the very best of luck with *Waterside Up*. I understand that he is already working on a sequel, to be called *Butterside Up*, which follows the fascinating story of a small shoal of smoked-salmon sandwiches. I can hardly wait.

Jogging from Memory

I always used to think that my age didn't matter to me, and I have often said that I could face any imminent birthday with equanimity provided I got a record token or a pair of socks. Friends, I was wrong. By the time you read this, I shall have celebrated my thirtieth birthday. I never thought that I would be worried by being thirty: but now that I am, I am. Very.

Traditionally, the beginning of the fourth decade of life is a time for review. It is a time for review of one's past achievements and review of one's dwindling potential for the future. Depending on how honest one is (and this particular one is not very), it is also a time for reviewing the enlarging potential for enlarging one's dwindly past achievements as one reviews them. In private I swore to myself that, come the day, I would not fall prey to maudlin introspection but would face the onset of senescence with a spiritual calm and tranquility. But that was before I took part in that damnable mass-jog.

Now I have nothing against mass-jogs: several of my best friends are joggers and a few of them celebrate mass. I have always said that what a man does in the early morning or late evening, even if it involves dressing up in peculiar clothes and doing a lot of heavy breathing, is his own affair. In fact, like most doctors brought up to believe in preventative medicine, I have always thought that a healthy diet and a bit of jogging would be the answer to most twentieth-century ills, *e.g.* heart disease, gallstones, loss of the ozone layer, lassa fever and global warfare. And of course, like most doctors brought up to believe in preventative medicine, I recommended it to all my patients and never tried it myself. You see I never thought I actually needed to (like most patients brought up not to believe in preventative medicine). As a matter of fact I thought I was pretty goddam fit, thank you very much. I reckoned that in the daily grind of my vigorous and demanding life I got plenty of exercise: things like humping around old anatomy textbooks, carting out my daughters' nappies (much the same thing as regards weight, content and artistic merit), lifting the dust-cover off my typewriter (a proper desk model, not one of those namby-pamby lightweight portables), and tearing up the little cards that appear through my letter-box advertising highly suspect roofing firms. Keeping myself in constant trim this way, I was fairly confident that if I were suddenly to be faced with some James Bond type of situation, such as wrestling with a Manta Ray or carrying Ursula Andress up a mountain (much the same thing as regards weight, content and artistic merit), I would be able to cope. I suppose I thought that I would just snap into it (or them) and that those rippling muscles of mine, honed and trimmed by years of patient work-out on the coffee percolator and Sunday papers, would carry me through the day. Came the day, they didn't. Came the day after, they wouldn't even carry me out of bed. And that in the closing hours of my twenty-ninth year.

It all seemed a jolly enough idea at the time. They rang me up and said, look, all these doctors are going on this jog and isn't that a good idea? And I said, yes, yes, a jolly enough idea (being a doctor brought up to believe in preventative medicine). And they said, it's a jog not a race and it only lasts thirty minutes and no matter how famous you are you should be able to survive thirty minutes of jogging, shouldn't you? And so, like most doctors brought up to believe in preventative medicine, I said, yes, yes, count me in, and privately hoped that the whole thing would be cancelled due to an earthquake or a plague of frogs. No such luck.

So that is why on a crisp Saturday morning, the day before my thirtieth birthday, I found myself on the athletics track of the big stadium at Crystal Palace (even the name gives me fibrositis now). I looked around me and saw three hundred assorted medics dressed in an extraordinary variety of jogging shorts (ranging from sub-Olympic silk slit-up-the-side things to ones made of material that I last saw on a deckchair). Most of us were trying to preserve the last vestiges of a hopelessly shrivelled dignity by standing around in clumps of three or four as if we were at a cocktail party at which someone had stolen all the drinks, canapés, peanuts and guests' clothing.

25

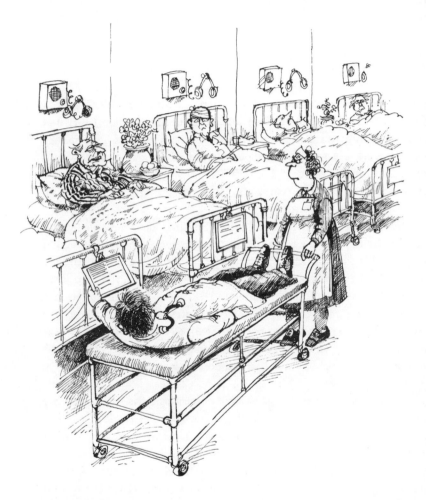

" I SEE THE DOCTOR'S BEEN OUT JOGGING AGAIN, SISTER".

A few of the more professional and athletic gentlemen were warming up, doing press-ups and some manoeuvres that looked a bit like post-natal pelvic floor exercises. I studied these activities from afar and thought that they looked like the sort of thing that I ought to be doing, but then realised that I didn't know how; so I pretended that I didn't want to. In the end I compromised by limbering up — well more like lumbering up, really — by running once round the track, followed by an intensive burst of callisthenic autograph-signing.

After ten minutes of all that, I was raring to go; or at least to go and have a warm shower and a little lie-down. But just then they gathered us all together at the starting-line, told us it was a jog and not a race, and, in the unfortunate absence of an earthquake or plague of frogs, fired the gun, and we were away. My first thoughts were to remind myself that this was not a race and that I should not burn out too early, but should pace myself for the whole jog; even so, we natural athletes are virtually unrestrainable, and within seven seconds of the start I was eleven yards down the track and already being lapped by a fell-walker and two marathon-runners.

After the first hundred yards I settled into my accustomed loping stride, or rather something that I hoped would look like my accustomed loping stride, though it was more a variation on a limp. I got into something like a steady rhythm and after one hour of nerve-wracking gut-splitting effort, I was surprised to hear the announcement over the public address system that we had been running for just under ten minutes. I took the opportunity to review my current status. My breathing was stertorous and had all the regularity of a drum solo by Buddy Rich with a sore finger. My left leg was undoubtedly developing early signs of *rigor mortis*. My right pectoral muscles seemed to be developing botulism, and I had a sneaking suspicion that my deltoids had caught Dutch Elm disease. Every other part of me was just fine except for incipient rabies. I noticed a strange white blur to my left and dimly wondered if it was one of those weird visual troubles that Amundsen's lot got at the Pole; but then I remembered that I hadn't eaten any polar bear liver, let alone too much, and that my recent exposure to a horizon white-out was pretty minimal. The white blur was actually caused by a steady stream of

27

runners overtaking me on the inside.

I have heard it said that on a long-distance run you have time to listen to the natural tunes and rhythms of your own body. I listened. What I heard suggested to me that my pericardium, the fine and delicate wrapping around my heart, was on fire. I could hear my muscles aching. In fact after nine laps I began to develop muscle pains in places where I didn't even have muscles. Everything hurt, even my toenails and eyelashes. Air suddenly seemed to be a commodity in short supply, if not actually out of stock. I seemed to be slowing down, as if running in treacle, an effect I attributed to the aerodynamic drag caused by the little paper number pinned to my shirt. In review, as I came into the last lap, my summary of the situation was that I was twenty-nine years old, thoroughly insane and unlikely to live to be thirty. Fifty yards from the end I rallied very slightly and regained my composure; I even saw a group of doctors who were scarcely twice my age and who had only lapped me six times. Not so bad for 29 after all, I thought. I crossed the finishing line with the style and grace of Landseer's 'Stag At Bay', though most people said it looked more like Picasso's 'Guernica' or even Van Gogh's 'Wooden Chair'. Nonetheless, I had jogged and I had survived; or so I was told.

And in the bar afterwards: my, what bravado and braggadocio there was! Were these my fellow crucifees now clustering round, eager with chatter and orders of slimline tonics, declaring to a man what fun and how bracing it all had been? And would I become one of them now? Would I turn hypocrite and lie through my teeth about how awfully super and jolly easy it had been? Of course I would. I mean, I don't mind looking a fool but there's no point in looking stupid as well, is there?

Back at the railway station it took me eight minutes to walk from the train to my motor-bike. Having got to it, I couldn't lift my foot high enough to kick-start it. The next day it took me fifteen minutes to get down the eight steps to the bathroom. Breathing seemed to be an exercise I didn't have enough breath for. Standing up was a luxury I forced myself to do without. Mind you, James Bond might have felt just the same the day after hauling Ursula Andress up the mountain. So might the Manta Ray. One just doesn't know.

And now, facing the truth at thirty, what next? Am I game for the next physical challenge to this ageing, crumbling frame? Of course I am. Let me make it quite clear that if I am invited to join another medics mass jog-in, I'll sign up at once. Provided I'm still 29, that is.

A Kick in the Monads

It is not generally known that Stalin was fond of the works of Leibniz. He once said (though it is often misquoted), 'When I hear the word revolver, I reach for my Leibniz.' And not surprising, either. For, of all the seventeenth-century Gothic philosophers, Leibniz was by far the most impenetrable. It has been calculated that to get through his entire collected philosophical works one would need nothing less than a 30mm armour-piercing shell. It was this fact that made Stalin feel safe from revolvers, since he carried the philosopher's complete works close to his heart, under his shirt. This not only protected him but also prevented him from going through doorways sideways, or turning over in bed.

However, apart from their bullet-proofing powers, Leibniz's rational systems have little to offer the modern-day homemaker: generally speaking, a Habitat catalogue is thinner, cheaper and more profusely illustrated. Born in Leipzig in 1649, Gottfried Wilhelm Freiherr von Leibniz went to university where he was often confused with *lebniz*, a sort of dark brown *croûton* fried in sump oil and thrown over the surface of cabbage soup, or small forest fires if there is nothing else handy. He was also confused with *lipnitz*, a Bavarian type of open sandwich comprising *bratwurst, hasselblad, brottbrattbludde* and *munchen gladbach*. In fact, Leibniz was often confused. Since he was a philosopher, this did not really matter very much, and nobody noticed.

From university he went to Nuremberg where he made the acquaintance of Baron von Boineburg, so called because his left leg was replaced by a steel spring like Zebedee in *The Magic Roundabout*. Boineburg introduced him to the Elector of Mainz, who confused Leibniz with the dark brown *croûtons* and tried to throw him over the surface of some cabbage soup. However, once it was all sorted out they found it was 1669, so they needed someone to promote the German claim to the vacant throne of Poland. You can see how dangerous it was to leave anything vacant in Poland when the Germans wanted to sit down. As I am certain you knew all the time, it was then that Leibniz wrote his pamphlet *Specimen Demonstrationum Politicarum Prorege Polonorum Eligiendo* — a catchy little number that the populace found they could whistle. In fact they had to, because they could not pronounce it. Anyway it failed, and a Polish prince got onto the vacant throne.

Our hero therefore directed his attention to defending Germany by persuading Louis XIV of France to attack Egypt. After that he spent the rest of the afternoon in the Tuileries where he met Huygens, the physicist. Under his influence, Leibniz studied mathematics and natural philosophy and did a Part II B.Sc. in differential calculus, safe cracking and long division. Now this was a time at which the leading intelligentsia of Europe were sinking into a philosophical quagmire. They were constantly asking each other vitally important questions such as 'What *causes* things?' 'If a white billiard ball strikes a red one,' they demanded, 'what is the *cause* of the movement of the red one? Is the spatial coincidence a necessary condition of the movement, or merely an epiphenomenon? Could the movement occur without it? Will it occur next time?' and so on. The seventeenth-century dualistic thinkers had not quite twigged that if a white billiard ball strikes a red one, and the red one then goes in off the top cushion, there is only one vitally important question to be asked, and that is 'How much have you got on the game?'

It was at this point, then, that Leibniz brought out his greatest rational system — monadism. The basic idea was that the whole world was made of particles called monads, which were the true seat of all prime causes. In his view, monads were all alike in that they were all seats of activity and were percipient, but they differed in quality. Just like a crowd at a horse-race — except that monads never gambled or dropped litter. The idea had a limited popularity among the intellectuals and one Venetian philosopher christened his eldest daughter Monad Lisa, but it never caught on among the populace. The basic problem was that the monads, as a group, being identical, percipient and self-active, seemed like a bunch of prissy goody-goodies. Since they were held to be the prime causes of everything that actually happened, they would have been an ideal scapegoat group if anything went wrong. ('It's them dang monads as is makin' the cattle die: saddle up, men, we'll git Spinoza and Locke along and invalidate 'em in the gulch.')

But what would have happened if monadism *had* caught on? It would have meant that every single event in every facet of every activity in the universe would be caused by — and therefore dependent on — the Leibniz monads. If Leibniz had ever called his monads out on strike, the whole universe would have come to a total standstill. Now you might ask why a man of Leibniz's character should ever have wanted the universe to come to a standstill. The answer is in the example of the billiard balls. Leibniz was actually a rotten billiard player and hated losing. The purpose of his whole rational system was to get the monads installed as the only true and final prime movers, and then to withold their labour while his opponent was having his shot; so that when the white ball struck the red, there being no prime cause, the red would not move. Then, when it was his turn, Leibniz would fish a monad out of his pocket, sink the red, and then go on to pot the black.

Faced with that kind of threat to democracy and the universal order of things, the world breathed an understandable sigh of relief when it read of Leibniz's death in 1717. He actually died in 1716 but the world was a slow reader in those days. Anyway the monads never enjoyed a revival and never even got an album of their greatest hits released. There was a rumour that the last few prime movers got jobs working for the Russian chess grand masters, but the rest gave up because there just weren't enough billiard balls in the world to give them all a job. Maybe that was Leibniz's problem all along — too many final causes and not enough balls.

Dreams of an Insomniac

Mnyeeownn-bonk-squeenk-squeenk-bonk — BLINK. Flight GW 350 from the Land of Nod has just landed. I blink and am awake. It is ten to four in the morning, and I am awake enough to realise that I have woken up asking myself the question: why am I waking up? Insomnia is a terrible thing. For a start, it stops you sleeping and as if that wasn't bad enough, well . . . well that *is* bad enough. And here I am again, awake in the small hours between dozing wife on one side and transmitted burps and farts of baby crackling down the baby-alarm on the other. A bad scenario, but, experienced insomniac that I am, I do not panic. The first thing I do is to try to pretend that I am asleep dreaming that I am awake. I got that idea from a novel I read once. As a never-fail method of getting back to sleep, it is a total failure. It never works.

The next thing I do is to run a total systems check, as airline pilots do, to see if there is any particular reason why I should have woken up. This takes time and expertise but brings great security of mind. Brain to bladder: systems check and status read-out, please: over. Roger, brain: bladder reads out five cms water pressure, here, micturition drive on auto-pilot at zero, warning lights are green, green and green, ETP is 0915: over. Roger, bladder: brain to bowel, status check: over. Roger, brain: bowel at zero tension right now: we will not evacuate unless alarm sounds continuously, rendezvous point is ramp outside car park 'D': nerve plexus tells us that bran biscuits haven't worked again: green, green and green: over. Roger, bowel: brain to genitals, over: repeat, brain to genitals, over: brain to pelvis, I cannot raise genitals, repeat cannot raise them, assume it wasn't them that woke us up then.

By now I am fully awake in charge of a sleeping nervous system. This is not a good situation since the absence of a specific fault implies the absence of a specific remedy. However the process so far has been composed of what the philosophers call analytic truths: if I do not feel randy, then the feeling of randiness does not exist, by definition. I now move on to what are called synthetic truths — notably, observations about the outside world. For instance (I ask myself), is the outside world on fire? Have I been woken up by the smell of burning? Am I being asphyxiated by dense clouds of lethal polystyrene furniture fumes? Have I, in fact, woken up dead? This is of course a philosophical question that can never be fully answered, since nobody can logically prove that they are not dead. Even collecting Supplementary Benefit is no proof of actual life as far as philosophers are concerned. I'm told that many social workers have much the same viewpoint too.

However, on this occasion, the house — synthetically speaking (which it is) — is not aflame. Listening to the world, I note that the streets are not resounding with civil commotion, riot, hostile action or anything else my insurance company will not tolerate. We are not under flood or subsidence (15% extra unless minimum cover is waived). I am however fully awake. I decide to get up, have a glass of water and waive my minimum cover. Risking flashing my uncovered — but somnolent — genitals at the bare streets, I dash across the landing to the bathroom. Looking at my image in the bathroom mirror does not produce the reassuring soporific effect that it usually has on my students during tutorials. Maybe this is because I wear clothes for tutorials (query: is it my dress sense that puts them to sleep then?).

I decide to try out a cure for insomnia that I read in *Reader's Digest* fifteen years ago. (One possible cure for insomnia is of course reading fifteen-year-old *Reader's Digests*, though I must add the caution that if you can't find any, the search for them will keep you awake.) It said that if you get out of bed and allow your body to get really cold, when you get back in the warmth will help you nod off. I turn on the extractor fan. This fan, installed by an over-enthusiastic electrician, is an industrial model designed to empty a ten-acre glue factory in the event of a fire. It is so powerful that not only does it extract any possible vestige of noisome odour from the bathroom but if there is anybody in the street walking past, it will blow their hat off. At four

"HE FINALLY FOUND A CURE FOR HIS INSOMNIA THEN?"

in the morning it sounds like Concorde and feels like Hurricane Betty. In the maelstrom of its cooling draught, I sit on the edge of the bath. I wonder what my wife would say if she could see me like this. Or the police. Though why the police should want to sit naked on the edge of my bath I do not know. As hypothermic coma begins to supervene, I crawl back to bed.

Gradually I begin to warm up, but not to nod off. What is insomnia, I ask. I do not know, I answer. Insomnia is no goddam use to anyone, I add, except . . . except to people who have to write pieces like this one. And just as I begin to think of writing this piece, I notice that I am fast asleep. My last thought is the faint worry that if thinking about *writing* this is so soporific, what's it going to be like actually reading it. Let me know when you wake up.

Listless in Gaza

Dear Doctor Freud,

I'm sorry to bother you again. I assume that things have been getting a bit hectic for you down at the old Vienna Royal Infirmary which is, I suppose, why you haven't had time to reply to my last letter. Anyway, I wonder if I might just pick your brains — only a little bit — about a very simple point. I'd be glad of even a yes or no answer if you can manage it.

All I want to know is: is it abnormal to make lists? And if it isn't, is it abnormal to make lists of lists? And if *that* isn't abnormal, is it abnormal to go and make lists of all the things that aren't on other lists? You see I'm getting a little worried. I began making orderly lists of things while I was a student, in order to help cope with life around me, but I now have the nasty feeling that my list-making activities have increased to such an enormous extent that they have largely replaced the life around me. In fact, I am beginning to find that list-making is an addictive, although non-toxic, substitute for every known human activity (apart from list-making). The only advantage it has is that there are no known side-effects (unless you count dementia or broken marriages).

I seem to have developed a compulsion to arrange everything I see or need to do in some sort of order; but then, instead of actually dealing with the things on the list, I just rearrange them in different orders on other lists. Perhaps I can best illustrate my quandary by telling you a bed-time story that I often tell to my children. Oh, excuse me:

List of children (in order of appearance):
1. Joanna
2. Susan

or, to put it another way:

List of children (in alphabetical order):
1. Joanna
2. Susan

Now I'm not saying that this is the final and total size of our family, because, to be quite frank, my wife and I have been thinking about . . . well let me put it like this:

List of existing plus intended children:
1. Joanna
2. Susan
3. ?

I think that illustrates two of my main problems. Firstly, I am getting increasingly irritated at lists that have a '?' instead of a definite entry next to a number; secondly, that particular '?' is there because my wife and I haven't got round to starting the third child as I spend all my time making lists instead of doing things, including the kind of things we need to do to start the third one (as a matter of fact they're the same sort of things we needed to do to start the first two, only more so).

I'm afraid I seem to have wandered off the point and I've been rambling on about sex — I do hope you don't think I'm mad or anything; of course you don't, do you? — but I did mean to tell you this bed-time story that I often tell my children (you can probably remember their names, can't you?).

It concerns a man who made lists of everything that he had to do, and wouldn't do anything unless it was on a list labelled 'Things To Do'. This went on all right for a long time but gradually he found that he was not only *unwilling* to do anything that wasn't on a list, but eventually became totally *unable* to do anything not on a list. Even that didn't matter very much until one day he lost his master list of Things To Do and found that he couldn't go to sleep at night, because he hadn't got a list with 'go to sleep' on it. Then he realised that he couldn't even look for his master list because there was no list anywhere saying 'look for your lost list'. So he couldn't do anything at all, and was forced to stand absolutely still staring at the floor doing nothing. After ten years, he was appointed chairmen of a large nationalised industry.

Of course the story is pure fiction — in real life it only takes two years of total inactivity to become chairman of a large nationalised industry — but it does point to some of the major difficulties confronting the list-maker.

My main difficulty is slightly different. I don't have any problems trying to do things that aren't on lists; I just find that putting things to do onto lists is much nicer than actually doing them. I first noticed this alarming habit when I was a student revising for my final examinations. I wrote out long lists on each subejct, listing the main topics that I thought I ought to mug up on. For example:

Pharmacology topics:
1. Antibiotics
2. Antihistamines
3. Steroids & Anti-inflammatory drugs
4. Other little white tablets
5. Secret of eternal youth

and so on. I accumulated hundreds of these lists but still did not actually get round to revising any of the topics. So I then made secondary lists, each of which listed the most important lists of topics that I hadn't revised. Two days before the exams I made one single master list of all the secondary lists, but still didn't manage to do any revision. The day before the exams I threw even that list away and wrote one list labelled:

Things to do tomorrow:
1. Pass exams

which somehow I managed to do.

I suppose that, in essence, I am one of those people who has never let life simply slip by me. I have listed every aspect, every feature and every factor of daily living, and *then* let it slip by me. I now find that I have so many lists on the go that it takes me all my time to keep them up to date. My method works in the following way. Suppose that I have five things I think I ought to do; I will start a list such as:

Things to do:
1. Pay electricity bill
2. Let Phil know about Friday — as usual!
3. Ring the regional office about the bloody tumble-drier
4. Get Derek to drop the specimens off at Roger's
5. Pay gas bill

As you can see, some of these things are highly unpleasant tasks, so I tend to do the ones I don't mind so much and transfer the nasty ones to another list:

Things to do now:

1. Pay electricity bill
2. Let Arnold know about Thursday
3. Get Charles to fix up other wash-basin
4. Check the fluorescein-conjugated lectins and the flow cytometer before testing the lactoperoxidase labels in the electron spin resonance chamber
5. Pay gas bill
6. Ring the *head* office about the bloody tumble-drier

and when I am left with a residue of things that haven't been done on that list, I start one with an even more urgent heading, such as:

Things to do RIGHT NOW!:

1. Pay electricity bill

and so the payment of the electricity bill works its way up from the next list, which is the THINGS TO DO PRONTO URGENT RIGHT AWAY NOW list, all the way to the ultimate URGENT EMERGENCY PANIC THINGS TO DO ABSOLUTELY PRONTO URGENT THIS MINUTE LAST CHANCE HURRY HURRY list. Which is when I start a brand new list:

Things to get my wife to do:

1. Pay electricity bill
2. Check the fluorescein-conjugated lectins and the flow cytometer &c &c

Well, dear Dr Freud, that's about the strength of the problem with me, and I'd be very glad to know if you can help in any way. To be quite honest I'm only writing to you now because my Emergency Pronto Panic Panic list happens to say:

1. Write to Dr Freud about lists.

I suppose it might all be due to over-enthusiastic toilet training. Anyway, I'd better stop now as my desk is cluttered with the makings of thousands of little lists, and I see that I have developed a particularly nasty one to starboard. Do drop me a line if you've got a moment,

Kind regards,
ROB BUCKMAN

Christmas Boxes

Every December, as I find myself buffeted along the brightly-lit streets of London's West End by happy, laughing, greedy, materialistic crowds, and as the nights draw in and the pavement artists draw on, I ponder the true meaning of the Christmas festival and despair of ever understanding its real significance. I have searched everywhere for the answer to this perennial spiritual enigma. I once asked the lady in the information booth at Selfridge's. She seemed to know the answer to every other question, so I enquired of her what the real significance of the Christmas celebration was. She said, 'Try "Leather Goods", dear.' I was too young then to understand what she meant. In fact, I still am.

I asked my mother the same question, but she misheard me and gave me the standard lecture that she had learned from the Family Doctor booklet on How Babies Are Made. As a matter of fact she also gave me the same lecture when I asked her about VAT, and now that I have experienced both, I see the similarity. I asked my Uncle Harry, who does something in the hotel business (usually stealing), and he said, 'My dear girl,' (his sight was failing, or possibly his memory) 'Christmas is nothing but an evil commercial invention of the capitalist consortiums to increase profits, and it would be a whole lot better if it came in February when business is very slack.'

So last year I set out to learn the real essence of Christmas for myself. As I ventured forth on this voyage of discovery, delving deep into the innermost crinkles of my psyche, I tried to be totally honest. After all, it was Christmas. I knew that deep down inside, I loved Christmas. But was it, I asked myself, merely because of the gaudy shops jammed with glossy novelties and bright cheap baubles? Was it merely the commercial spirit and the profit motive that so lifted my heart? Was it merely the exchange of monies and the tinkling of cash

41

registers that made me look forward to Christmas from Boxing Day onwards? And I answered: yes, it was. Christmas is the time when the Spirit of Giving is everywhere in evidence, and if there is one thing I enjoy more than all others, it is to allow other people to enjoy themselves by giving me lots of presents. I know that in so doing I deny myself the Pleasure of Giving on my own account, but no true joy comes without sacrifice.

But then I carried my self-exploration a step further. Granted that Christmas signifies the widespread joy of others in giving me gifts, what is the most enjoyable aspect of the Christmas shops? (If, by the way, you liked the quiz questions in the transfusion section of this book, I'll slip a few into this one. And if you didn't, I won't.) What then is the single feature, so unique to the Christmas shops, that brings such rare happiness to the aching heart? (That was Quiz Question Two. What more do you want? That was Question Three.)

My quest took me to my most favourite of all shops, the book-shop. And while musing upon a pile of new and glossy Christmas releases in a gay and brightly-lit modern bookshop, I stumbled across a rather strange book. It told a simple tale of a child born in an animal's manger in a stable, because there was no room at the inn for the mother and putative father. The book came in a plain but stout and shiny cardboard slip-case, which also held another book telling of the creation of the whole world and of the first man and woman in it.

And then the answer came to me. I suddenly realised that I was holding in my hands the two books and the slip-case which held the key to the real essence of Christmas. The real essence of Christmas is, it came to me in a flash of revelation, THE BOXED SET. All over the world, to worshippers of every creed, colour, language and credit card, Christmas means that special time of year when their favourite volumes are miraculously transmogrified and wrapped, bound in identical spines and glittering with uniform lettering, in glistening cellophane inside a festive and shiny case. Can there be anything more satisfying to the spirit? (That was Question Four. Clue: the answer is 'No'.)

But let us progress yet a step further into our study of the human soul at Yuletide. Let us ask ourselves what it is about the boxed set that exerts such miraculous and so seasonal a pull? (This is the only

" WELL, IF HE HAS LOST THE BOXED SET WE'LL JUST HAVE
TO MAKE DO WITH THE GOLD, FRANKINCENSE AND MYRRH.

quiz where you ask the questions yourselves. You'll find it less menacing that way.) Well, first of all, and above all, a boxed set of books is substantial. If someone gives you the Gormenghast trilogy or the Orwell diaries it tells you something about the donor straight away. It tells you that they were prepared to spend three (or even four) times as much money on you as they would have if they had bought you only a single book. Unless of course they stole the set; but even then the enlarged bulk increases their chance of getting caught and so magnifies the value of their gift and/or theft.

Secondly, the boxed set appeals to two basic human emotions simultaneously — the desire to read, learn and inwardly digest, and the desire to collect things in sets. In the event of a clash, the latter usually wins out over the former. You pick up the box and you become imbued with a sense of impending scholarship. You say to yourself, yes, yes, I will go home and make a cup of tea, and I will begin at the first page of the first volume and continue through the set to the last page of the last volume, and I will be improved by the experience. And if not, at least I'll enjoy the cup of tea.

Of course the book industry, being steeped in theology ever since Thomas Aquinas and *Das Kapital,* has appreciated the deeper meaning of Christmas for many years. Thus not only are special boxed sets of the Testaments widely available, but for years there have been special Christmas sets of C. S. Lewis's Narnia stories, of Proust's *Remembrance of Things Past* and of Powell's *Dance To The Music Of Time.* All this I can understand. I can see why publishers should put a set of House and Garden Improvement books together in one box, or a set of dictionaries of English, music and quotations, or even half-a-dozen great ghost novels or murder stories. But lately the true spirit of Christmas has been adulterated and cheapened. Publishers have denigrated and desecrated the sanctified task of boxing together in one place those that belong together, and have been shacking up in a box a collection of volumes that are merely casual acquaintances rather than life-long soul-partners. Such promiscuity may be justified from a commercial and mercenary point of view, but I say that it is not Christmas as the true book-buyer knows it.

Nowadays, for instance, one sees boxes labelled with things like 'The Goodbye Books — Five Great Books With The Word Goodbye

In The Title: *The Long Goodbye, Goodbye to Berlin, Goodbye Mr Chips, Goodbye To All That*, and *Good Buys In Double Glazing.'* (That was actually the complete answer to Question Nineteen but we never got there. Sorry.) What justification could there be, I say, for a boxed set called 'The Doctor's Bedside Manner Box', comprising *Doctor Zhivago, Doctor Doolittle, Doctor No, Doctor Jekyll and Mr Hyde, Doctor In The House*, and *Doctor's Dilemma.* I mean if that isn't prostitution, then what is? (That was Question Five. I hope none of you knows the answer.)

Or what about the box called 'The Voyager's Set Of Italian Towns', including *The Turin Shroud, Death in Venice, Two Gentlemen of Verona, A Woman Of Rome*, and *Florence* (actually a biography of Florence Nightingale). You can now get something called 'Birds In Literature' cobbled together from Aristophanes's *The Birds* plus *The Seagull, The Wild Duck, One Flew Over The Cuckoo's Nest* and *Sparrows Can't Sing.* There is even a measure of cross-fertilisation as a sign of the final degradation of this once wonderful celebration. For instance *The Long Goodbye* pops out of 'The Goodbye Books' and appears in 'The Long Books', together with *Long Day's Journey Into Night, Loneliness of the Long Distance Runner*, and *The Long Way To Tipperary* (wrongly translated in the Japanese editions as 'The Wrong Way To Tip A Lady'). Then *Death In Venice* crops up alongside *Death In The Afternoon, Death On The Nile* and *Death of a Salesman*, as 'The Coroner's Christmas Bedside Box'. What is the world coming to? (Question Six.)

Well, as the striptease artiste said to her costumier, everything changes but everything is the same. Christmas will continue to be Christmas no matter what is wrapped up in cardboard slip-cases, and thems as don't like it, can lump it. I hope, though, that after you have read this and understood my viewpoint, that your attitude to Christmas will have changed just a little bit. At least you will know what to buy for me, won't you? (That was Question Seven.)

The End of the Peer

I wish to make public a solemn and awesome declaration which will be binding on me for the rest of my life. It is this: I shall never make public any solemn and awesome declaration that will be binding on me for the rest of my life. Now this isn't the simple and common terror of written agreements that most people get after they've been to an estate agent's; this is an anxiety complex that I acquired all by myself when I was a kid. Just like the grown-ups always said: it was all due to the comics I was reading.

When I was about eight years old I inherited my brother's collection of *Classics Illustrated* comics. They were — and may still be — comic-book format versions of great works of literature, such as 'Hamlet', 'Lorna Doone', 'Jekyll and Hyde' and so on. My favourite of all was the *Classics Illustrated* version of Dickens' 'A Tale Of Two Cities'. I spent a great deal of time looking at that particular comic and it wasn't until I was nineteen that I realised that Dickens hadn't drawn the pictures, but had merely written the original story. When I had heard people talking of Dickens as 'a great writer', I had always assumed that they were referring to his ability to fit his characters' speeches neatly and legibly into the white balloons coming out of their mouths. Anyway, one of the more graphic scenes in 'Two Cities' etched itself very deeply on my impressionable and putty-like brain and gave me the complex to which I have referred.

The story concerned an old man who had been imprisoned by the Aristocrats, who had also done something awful, like poisoned his wife. While in prison he wrote a solemn and awesome declaration, stating that he would never rest until every single Aristocrat was beheaded or at least imprisoned for life and charged double VAT. After many years of incarceration he was rescued by La Revolution and became one of their most popular heroes. It then transpired that his daughter had married an Aristocrat and that his poor son-in-law was in the hands of La Revolution. Naturally they found a copy of the old man's solemn and awesome declaration and read it out at the son-in-law's trial, which made the tribunal ever so shirty about the whole thing. The upshot was that the son-in-law was carted off to La Bastille when everyone agreed that a clever lawyer could have got him off with a fine and an endorsed driving licence. *Now read on.*

The point of the episode — as I saw at the age of eight — was that you should never make solemn and awesome declarations that will be binding on you for the rest of your life. Or if you do, you shouldn't put them in writing. Or if you do put them in writing, you shouldn't let your daughter marry an Aristocrat. Or if she does, you shouldn't let them live in France in the eighteenth century. Now the trouble is that, having a tidy mind, there is one solemn and awesome declaration that I have always wanted awesomely to declare. I have always wanted to state that I shall never practise private medicine on my own account (although I have no objection to any of my comrades or colleagues doing so). The few people to whom I have divulged this awesome declaration were so impressed that they nicknamed me 'Awesome Welles'. Now I do foresee the possibility of my daughter marrying a private patient. Nevertheless, I cannot rid myself of the desire to make my declaration, even if they read this book out loud at my son-in-law's trial. (They may as well since it's never going to feature on the BBC's 'Book At Bedtime', is it?)

My objection to private medicine is based purely on the fact that I cannot manage to maintain a normal doctor-patient relationship when I know I'm dealing with a paying customer. The knowledge that money will be changing hands upsets my usual equanimity and makes me feel like a fumbling shop assistant. I feel that I ought to be bringing down two dozen shoe-boxes filled with different diagnoses and schemes of treatment and offer them to the patient. As I say, it's a purely personal feeling, but it started with the very first private patient that I was asked to see, and has been with me since.

The first private patient I saw was a retired Lord who had drunk himself into fairly advanced cirrhosis in some duty-free haven or other; he would get himself flown to England periodically to see my boss, the Consultant, and have himself sorted out. He (the Lord) was a

47

very tall and incredibly Aristocratic old man with a remarkably charismatic aura. He commanded instant obedience, like a male Lady Bracknell.

Even doing something as simple as taking a blood sample from him made me feel like an acolyte attending Thomas à Becket. In fact, not knowing how to address a Lord, I think I actually called him 'Your Grace' a couple of times. I don't think he minded. Or even noticed. Anyway, my boss asked me to take a small specimen of his Lordship's liver for analysis (a procedure known as liver biopsy), and although I was quite confident about my ability to do the job, I found myself behaving in an incredibly deferential and grovelly manner. This manifested itself as a tendency to make bad and nervous jokes. As I started off, I heard myself say, 'I'll just swab down the skin with some iodine-in-alcohol. You're not allergic to iodine, are you? Well at least we know you're not allergic to alcohol. Ha! ha!' His Lordship was not amused. A few seconds later I was horrified to hear myself twittering on as follows: 'This is the local anaesthetic. I'll use the full 10ml — you can afford the extra tuppence, can't you? Ha! ha!' Despite all the *faux pas,* I performed the liver biopsy beautifully and went back the next day to tell him he could get out of bed. He called me over in his 'instant obedience' voice, just like Trevor Howard in *Charge of the Light Brigade.* 'I say,' he barked, 'help me stand up, will you?' I did so and turned to go, when he called out, 'Heng awn a minute. I want to hev a pee.'

Personally I have never regarded helping a patient with this sort of thing as part of the after-sales service of the liver biopser, so I said that I'd get a nurse to give him a hand. But he said no, he wanted me to help him by holding the bottle in position for him. Wondering whether he had problems affecting his hands, I asked him why he needed assistance; his reply is etched forever on my memory. 'I want yew to heold the bottle becaws I need beoth my hends to heold my buttocks becaws otherwise when I pee, I fart. D'ye see?' I did see. I picked up the bottle and crouched down to plop it over his Aristocratic member, while he stood upright and clutched his bum. Things got underway and his Lordship got quite chatty, which unfortunately destroyed his concentration on the matter in hand. For as he rabbited on, he gradually loosened his grip on his buttocks.

"NO NURSE, THERE'S A BOX OF CHAMPAGNE CORKS THAT WE USE FOR OUR PRIVATE PATIENTS"

'Yes,' he said, 'it's quite a pleasant flight neow that they eonly stop at the Ilo de Sal PBSFLLT but the trouble is at my age THSSFLLTHTT any long journey is such a FSSLLTHTHPBT nuisance because if you sit still for more than a WHMMMOHSSTHT harf en hour or so THPPUPPARPPFST something goes wrong at either one end PPRRPPFRWHHWTP or the other, don't you know? THWOOPHLLFT.' I did know.

And that's what gave me my complex. I don't think I shall ever forget what it felt like to be crouching there, holding a rapidly warming bottle, with a cirrhotic belted Earl farting in my ear. And so I feel compelled to make my awesome declaration about private practice, despite my better judgement and despite the remote possibility of endangering the future prospects of any son-in-law of mine. Well, if my daughter does marry a private patient, he'll just have to find somebody else's ear to fart in. Sorry about that, but that's the way it is. I have declared.

What Heidegger Did Next

This is another example of my new collection of literary gems and philosophical reflections, 'The Moving Finger Handbook'.

There can be few philosophers who have had a greater impact on the philosophy of existence than the German genius Martin Heidegger. Most modern thinkers agree that in order to grasp the full meaning of his immense and complex work *Sein und Zeit* (Existence and Being) it is absolutely necessary to understand the mood of the times in which it was written, although fortunately it is not absolutely necessary to read it.

In simple terms, those philosophers who have contributed to the existentialist school have done so by considering the problem of the very essence of existence itself. In wondering what it actually means to exist, they addressed themselves to the question 'What *is*?' The so-called 'naivist' school answered that question by saying, 'What is what?', and pointed out that 'What is?' is ungrammatical. This led to a major split in the existentialist camp, with most of the naivists leaving to become hairdressers (among whom, to this very day, the comment 'What is what?' is regarded as the ultimate in wit and culture).

The second major phase of the existentialist philosophy began with a more detailed and objective examination of the different kinds of existence. Thus, one philosopher might say, 'Here is an apple. What is the essence of being an apple?' One group attempting to answer this problem were the Viennese purposivists. They replied by posing another question, 'What is the *point* of being an apple?', and then added the logical corollary that the point of being an apple could only matter to an apple, and that as a hypothetical postulate this was no way for grown men to spend their time. The concretists (based in Geneva) put it even more simply. 'Here is an apple,' they said, 'let us make dumplings.' However at the fifth international symposium on 'The Problem of Being' held in Paris in 1921, the concretists were

51

unanimously rejected by the assembly as a bunch of deviant heretics, although they won the Gold Medal in the hall next door for their dumplings.

The most unusual approach to the existentialist apple question was engineered by the negationists who set about systematically modifying the very matrix in which all ontological postulates (i.e. statements about existence) were made. Thus, their viewpoint could be expressed as 'This is not an apple. It's an elephant.' This led to a dramatic realignment of all the schools of existentialism, with the eventual emergence of the negationist-purposivists ('What is the point of being an elephant? Particularly if you're an apple.'), the negationist-concretists ('This is not an apple. It's a concrete-mixer.'), and of course the negationist-concretist-purposivists ('Let's make concrete dumplings.').

This, then, was the state of the art at the time of Heidegger's first explorations into these problems. Brilliantly he swept aside the entire muddle of existence (without actually killing himself) and asked the more fascinating question: 'If something that exists is an object that *is*, then what is the act of *not-being* — in other words, what does nothing do?' At first this was widely misinterpreted as the easier question 'What does nothing?'. To which, of course, the simple-minded electrivists said 'a broken vacuum-cleaner does nothing and a freezer in a power cut does nothing.' Some critics of philosophy, particularly those who resented the way Heidegger had been influenced by Kierkegaard, despite being unable to spell his surname or find out what his first name was, went so far as to say, 'Martin Heidegger does nothing.' These rather petty remarks were taken up and amplified by the glutealists who said, 'Martin Heidegger *is* nothing: nothing but a pain in the arse.'

Heidegger suffered this barrage with typical stoical calm. He continued his search for the act of non-being and after many years of experiment finally crystallised his answer to 'What does nothing do?' as 'Nothing noths'. Semeiologically speaking this was a bombshell, and as many of the phenomenologists said at the time, 'This is when the poo hits the fan.' For, by the simple act of inventing the transitive verb 'to noth', Heidegger not only offended the main body of ontologists by side-stepping their impasse, but also infringed the main tenets of logical positivism and broke several bye-laws of Berlin concerning spitting in trams and illegal fishing.

The implications of Heidegger's device were soon seen to be widespread. If nothing could truly be said to noth, then 'nothing' could be defined — in retrospect of course — as something that had nothed. But, by the same token, if we are examining at the present a single nothing that has, in the past, nothed and that will, in the future, noth again, we may legitimately ask exactly what it is doing now. The answer of course is simply that 'this particular nothing is now nothing.' This proposition can be treated mathematically, for if you divide through by the lowest common multiple, and then integrate with respect to time within the limits of twice and four times the half-life, you end up with 'nothing is nothing', plus a whole bag of 'this's' and 'is's' and other bits and bobs which you can use later on while the coffee is warming up.

Within a few years the concept of 'nothing is nothing' became rapidly established in all schools of philosophy and in all walks of life. It was adapted at the retail outlets of no less than eight supermarket chains as 'nothing is for nothing', an epigram that not only encapsulates the purpose of non-being but is also sound commercial sense and discourages shop-lifting. By the mid-50s no less than two hundred people had been prosecuted for stealing under Heidegger's fifth corollary of non-existence. Of those two hundred, eighty claimed in court that they were existentialists. The rest all claimed that they were Martin Heidegger.

His views stimulated the now famous Cologne group to put forward the legendary immortalist theory. The basic idea was that since Heidegger had so perfectly enshrined all the various facets of existence, if he died the whole world would suddenly cease to exist. They published a slim monograph on the subject which sold very well, and they used the royalties to organise a rota of fifty-two philosophers who sent Heidegger a 'Keep Well Soon' card every week. They also took out a massive insurance policy on his life, with the planet Earth quoted as beneficiary. After a vast amount of money had been paid in as premiums, it was then pointed out that the Cologne group were not true positivist existentialists of the immortalist school, but were actually con-men.

Perhaps the most revealing comment on Heidegger was written by his erstwhile colleague, now Professor of Unnatural Philosophy at Munich, Saul Reisenschein. Reisenschein suggested that Heidegger had been continually underrated: 'Without Heidegger' he wrote 'it would be impossible to do nothing. With him nothing is all you can · think about.'

As for myself, I have delved as deeply as I can into his famous and complicated works. I have read and re-read as much as is possible of 'Existence and Being' and after a while I suddenly realised, as I reached page five for the eighth time, the true essence of Heidegger's thought. It is totally incomprehensible. I therefore decided to telephone him and ask the one question that every philosopher the world over must have wanted to ask him: 'What *is* all this stuff about?' With considerable anxiety I dialled his number, and could hardly believe my luck when the phone at the other end was picked up and I heard his voice. Quavery with age and wisdom, his voice sounded strangely like that of a young girl, and although surprised I came out with my carefully rehearsed opening gambit. 'I would like to speak to Martin Heidegger,' I said, hoping in that one sentence that I was revealing myself as a lapsed logical positivist with a leaning towards but uncommitted to (by use of the conditional 'would') the mainstream existentialists. The reply took my breath away. 'Who?' the voice said. The genius of that simple interrogative stunned me into silence for a moment. Only a man of Heidegger's assurance in his own existence could demand, at the outset of an interview, a formal re-affirmation of that very self-existence. It was a game and I was falling for a Fool's Mate in the opening move. I rallied rapidly, and put forward a single postulate to which either response could only be a non-empty sub-category of the major premise. 'Is Martin Heidegger there?' I said, trembling. I was totally unprepared for the deserved *coup de grace*. After an electric silence, he said simply, 'No.'

The true essence of not-being came down the line at me with the full force of its creator, fresh and vigorous as ever. Heidegger had finally come full circle and had reconciled the essence of non-being with his own existence, to the subjugation of the latter. I could think of nothing (forgive the *double entendre*) to add to this gem and while I remained silent, the telephone connection, as if realising the perfect symmetry of the non-existence cycle, went dead. It took me weeks to recover.

And as for the future: will Heidegger ever really gain that pre-eminence among all philosophers that he truly deserves? Perhaps his future is best expressed in those words of Professor Reisenschein, 'Nothing doing'. No one could say fairer than that, could they?

Type Casting

My friend Doug is what modern-day psychiatrists would call a real Type A personality — the kind that perpetually dashes around the world developing jet-lag and ulcers. In fact one evening he came round and said he'd got jet-lag coming down from Manchester. I pointed out that since jet-lag was a biological disturbance caused by air travel between two places in different time zones, the journey from Manchester, which used Greenwich Mean Time like all of us, was unlikely to have caused it. Especially since he'd come down by train. Nonetheless, Doug is a typical Type A, and we were talking about the Type A personality at dinner the other night.

The usual gang were round our dinner table — Peter Ustinov, Ken Tynan, David Frost, David Owen, a few Previns, Oscar Wilde, Terry and Jean from No. 16, and James Boswell sitting in the corner developing writer's cramp. It was actually quite difficult to explain to non-medical people exactly what is meant by the Type A personality. David (Owen) began by defining it as one of the factors which markedly increases somebody's chance of having a heart attack, and adding that it should therefore be possible to identify the Type A personalities as a group of people most of whom were dead. I pointed out that this definition would also include a large number of other groups — the Tolpuddle Martyrs, the seventeenth-century metaphysical poets and anybody who was married to Henry VIII, for instance. David (Frost) interrupted simply in order to agree with me, and then Ken pointed out that we all knew exactly what we were talking about but couldn't define it. This, as he said, was a problem carefully explored by Wittgenstein, and subsequently inverted by the VAT inspectors who can define everything exactly, but don't know what they are talking about. After the laughter died down (0.03 sec) we all tried to think of one single activity that would encapsulate and define the true Type A — the obsessive, competitive, aggressive, repressed ego.

Oscar had first crack — as you'd expect — and said, 'It sounds to me as if the Type A personality is someone who flushes the toilet before finishing peeing.' As a definition, that seemed to be an excellent candidate for the Lowest Common Multiple of the Type A, until Terry from No. 16 pointed out its inherent sexism. The flushing-before-finishing concept might well define a Type A in a man, but in a woman, it would define a contortionist. Albeit a Type A female contortionist.

The next person to chip in was someone with a very vague idea of anatomy and physiology — I think it was Sir Peter Hall actually; he'd crept in to clear the coffee cups, but he has a habit of butting in on other people's conversations. He asked whether it was possible that Type A women faced the same way as men while peeing. None of us knew for certain, but one of the Previns said that there was a rumour that inside the Royal College of Psychiatrists the signs on the toilets had been changed from 'Ladies' and 'Gentlemen' to 'Type A' and 'Type B'. In the absence of confirmatory data, we dismissed this line of speculation as idle — if not actually hazardous to public health.

It was then that I came up with my great theory, but unfortunately by this time poor old Boswell had had to go to casualty for a wrist-splint, so I am forced to tell you all about it myself. It is my suggestion that the Type A personalities can be defined as the kind of people who have stickers in the back windows of their cars. Now, as a way of exhibiting the personality, the car sticker has a relatively short history. It began humbly enough in the post-war years with the dully informative RUNNING IN — PLEASE PASS and the self-evident TOGETHER WE CHOSE A MORRIS. Soon, though, the sticker began to grow more assertive and aggressive with cries such as YES! YET ANOTHER WALDORF SALOON FROM FELSTEIN'S OF KETTERING, and the race was on.

Travel was the next area of competition for the Type A stickers with things like WE HAVE SEEN THE LIONS OF LONGLEAT. Of course a *really* aggressive egocentric Type A would have proclaimed THE LIONS OF LONGLEAT HAVE SEEN US; but even without that form of extremism, the Type As were soon telling us that they had been to THE SEYCHELLES — ANOTHER WORLD and that we should imitate them and FLY CONCORDE — FLY THE FLAG. At this stage of my career, the only truthful thing I could have proclaimed from my back window would have been that I HAVE BEEN SICK IN A HOVERCRAFT.

The next phase was the sporty one. This began innocently enough with ROWING — A GROWING SPORT; but then came the very worrying and highly ambiguous exhortation PLAY RUGBY — FEEL A MAN! Obviously a lot more went on in the showers than we non-players suspected. The following stage was decidedly fruity. We were told that KITE FLIERS KEEP IT UP LONGER and that SURFERS DO IT STANDING UP; and as these declarations of minority preferences proliferate, it can't be long before we see MORRIS DANCING — PULL ANY OF THEM, THEY'VE ALL GOT BELLS ON.

And then, quite suddenly, the whole tone of the sticker changed from the suggestive and proclamatory to the imperative. I think it started with MARPLES MUST GO, but even after he'd gone the barking tone of the sticker stayed. Driving around a city was like being a lone rookie in a parade of sergeant-majors. It was all orders. I was told to SAY NO TO NUCLEAR ENERGY. I did so. I was ordered to GET OUT OF NORTH BORNEO NOW! Since I was, at the time, on a Honda 50 in Tottenham Court Road I found this an instruction easy to obey. Lately however the orders and exhortations have been getting increasingly esoteric and incomprehensible. STOP THE CROUCH END BOX sounds like something a Bow Street runner might have shouted on a bad night in Muswell Hill. I might have wanted to FREE THE FINCHLEY FOUR if I'd known what they'd done or if I'd been given a plan of the prison and a list of visiting times, but I had no idea why I should BLOCK THE ENFIELD AMENDMENT. Or indeed, how.

It may have been my paranoia but I began to feel that the stickers were becoming more and more personal. At any moment I expected to see one saying STOP SQUEEZING YOUR SPOTS or asking WHY DIDN'T YOU HAVE YOUR BOWELS OPEN THIS MORNING? One of the many questions concerning the human predicament more easily asked than answered. I retaliated against the Type As with a

"SHE HATES WINDOW STICKERS".

very simple device. I plastered the back of my motorbike with a fluorescent orange sticker bearing in three-inch black letters the simple legend BAN ALL STICKERS. I then wrote a letter to *The Times* suggesting that British Leyland design a new range of cars without back windows. I gave it all up after I'd persuaded my friend Dave to put three BAN ALL STICKERS stickers in his car, which so obscured his rear vision that he reversed over my motorbike.

I guess the truth is that I am such a modest sort of guy that I just hate telling people things and giving orders. Since nobody listened when I asked them to BAN ALL STICKERS, I don't suppose anybody will take any notice when I tell them to FINISH THIS SENTENCE AND TURN THE PAGE AT ONCE.

Hi-Fi with my Little Ear

Experts can get right up your nose. And now, thanks to modern technology, they can get right into your ears as well. I'm talking about the world of hi-fi stereo which has been playing very hard to get lately. I suppose it's the same with any science in its infancy (e.g. war or medicine), but recent hi-fi miracles have been wrapped in a veil of incomprehensible mysticism and described in a jargon unmatched for unintelligibility since Milton Friedman.

Let me say at the start that I have always been a bit of a hi-fi freak myself. As a schoolboy I used to save up my pocket-money to buy the American hi-fi magazine *Playboy*, and would spend hours drooling over its photographs of glossy amplifiers and sleek speakers. I think there were some boys in my class who bought *Playboy* for entirely different reasons — apparently the short stories and the interviews were highly thought of — but they were ignored by us purists.

After the time I'd spent looking at all that equipment worth $2000 and more, I must say that I found my very first gramophone was a bit of a come-down. It was called the Dansette 'Bermuda' and cost £17, and all it did was play records, smell of warm plastic and look fairly tidy in two-tone grey.

Actually, now that I think about it, the fantasy world conjured up by *Playboy* made several aspects of reality look a bit dreary by comparison: I seem to remember that my very first girlfriend was not a long-legged blonde, did not have perfect teeth or even a staple in her navel. But to be fair, she *did* play records, did smell of warm plastic and looked fairly tidy in grey (her school uniform), so I couldn't really grumble. By complete coincidence her name was also Dansette Bermuda and she had a younger brother called Ferguson. However, I digress.

The point is that the true hi-fi freak looks upon a Dansette

Bermuda in the same way Barry Sheene looks upon a hoola-hoop. Simple to operate, but unrewarding. All it did (the 'Bermuda') was to play the record while you listened to the tune. After a time the limitations of the system grated somewhat and I got fed up with listening to a Concertgebouw orchestra that sounded as if it was playing inside a tin bath at the bottom of a disused mine-shaft.

So, a couple of years ago, I 'upgraded the system' (a technical hi-fi phrase meaning 'parted with three times the amount of money intended'). What I ended up with was, according to the salesman, the hi-fi equivalent of a Mercedes-Benz, though I now realise it was merely a Hillman Imp with new seat-covers. Anyway, the upgrading process left me with the feeling that I had gained some considerable expertise, since the experts had got so far up my nose as to imprint themselves on my frontal lobes. So while in expansive mood recently I bought a few modern hi-fi magazines, because I wanted to keep in touch and because the shop had sold out of *Playboy*. I was astonished to find that in just two years the whole hi-fi world had moved on without me. Latest developments clearly showed that my hi-fi system was less than half a notch above the old Dansette Bermuda, and had the re-sale value of the old hoola-hoop.

For a start, it was no longer the done thing to put on a record and listen to the tune. Oh no, nowadays there are at least eighty-one other things that have to be listened to first. Some of them are fairly easy to understand: for instance, it can't be that difficult to listen to the turntable (which produces 'rumble'). Similarly it must be fairly easy to listen to the amplifier: after all, the amplifier is the bit with the 'volume', 'bass' and 'treble' knobs which, with a bit of judicious twiddling, can make almost any orchestra sound like the Concert-gebouw in a tin bath down a mine-shaft.

My difficulties started when I read that one particular tuner (radio) had 'excellent low-level ambience cohesion' but gave 'a shade too much splash on transients'. How do you listen to *that*?

From there on, my credulity took an all-time basting. On the next page, a critic actually reviewed the sound of two turntable mats — one made of tacky plastic and one made of glass. He could distinguish the 'bass extinction and lack of tonal accuracy' that were improved by the glass mat. Or caused by it, I forget. Two pages

"A LOT OF THE DOCTORS AROUND HERE ARE STEREO FREAKS".

further on, another critic fully evaluated the sound of a new kind of connecting cable compared to which 'ordinary cables were muffled and gave a less open sound'.

I read no more. Suffering acute intellectual indigestion and flatulence, I gave a much more open sound of my own and rushed upstairs to my hi-fi Hillman Imp. I put a record on and listened very hard to detect the distortions due to the tone-arm bias compensator, the cartridge mount, the record-cleaning brush and the speaker cabinet veneer. The music sounded like this: *pya-dadda-POM paduddidi-FATAM*; but then it always had. But now I was worried. Was that *didi* of the *paduddidi* a true tonal harmonic or was it lacking in upper-mid-range definition? Was there thinness of the mid-band? And if there was, was there meant to be? Should I bash out another £800 merely to read afterwards that the London Philharmonic were renowned all over the world for the thinness of their mid-band, and had collected many gold medals for the thin *didis* in their *paduddidis*.

By the end of the afternoon I had convinced myself that I could hear the glue in the speaker cabinets. I was certain that I could detect flattening of the treble roll-off, brought about by too much machine oil on the amplifier on-off switch. I could hear the rubber feet on the cassette-deck. I could sense the mid-bass distortion caused by my daughter's Marmite fingerprints on the tuner dial.

And then, very suddenly, I recognised that feeling of aural paranoia and panic in a flash of *déjà vu*. It was just like being a medical student and told to listen to a special heart murmur. I remember standing there with the stethoscope in my reddened ears, hearing nothing more than a random collection of squeaks, whistles and thumps above the roaring of blood in my head, and being told that I was actually listening to the pre-systolic accentuation of a mid-diastolic murmur. The hell I was. I was probably listening to the label on my underpants.

That discovery has been of great comfort to me. I find it highly reassuring that hi-fi and medicine have so much in common. Apart from the fact that medicine is slightly cheaper, the nonsensical jargon, the bull and the obvious lying are exactly the same. So nowadays, if my houseman misses a heart murmur, I don't shout at him. I just tell him that his stethoscope is probably one of those that always gives a shade too much splash on transients. And I treat heart disease by asking the patient to sleep on a tacky plastic mattress (or a glass one) and to get their house rewired. I mean, we experts have got to keep ahead, haven't we?

A Strong Wind
in the Balearics

I know that I have my limitations and that I am merely mortal, but nothing in the world makes me more acutely aware of my limitations and makes me feel *more* merely mortal than listening to 'Round Britain Quiz' on the radio. 'Round Britain Quiz' is quite an unusual quiz show in that it is exceptionally and unashamedly highbrow, exquisitely polite, elegant and refined; it is English beyond the wildest dreams of Wodehouse. It is also completely unintelligible. I must have listened to at least forty programmes of it, and I can honestly say that I have never understood one single question, answer, explanation or riposte. I enjoy it enormously, but it does give me the sneaking suspicion that the contestants and the questioners have The Gift of Tongues. Or at least, that I don't.

Only the rules are simple. There are two teams — one consisting of a lady called Irene Thomas and a man called John Julius Norwich, and the other consisting of two other highbrow residents of whichever bit of Round Britain has volunteered to be Quizzed. Each team sits with its own chairman who gives them the questions, and simultaneously marks their answer, subtracting marks from a very English maximum of three points, depending on how many clues he has to give. One of the chairmen is Gordon Clough and his rather reassuring newsreader-type voice adds enormously to the impression that, in order to understand any of it, I would need an extra lobe in my brain. This is what it tends to sound like to me:

CLOUGH: Well now, Irene and John Julius, here's your question. What kind of trio would you get from a blob of pistachio, the 13th letter of the alphabet, and a strong wind in the Balearics?
NORWICH: Well, I say. This is very difficult.
THOMAS: I'll say it is.

NORWICH: Oh, dear. I haven't got a clue. *(Short pause — to try and convince listeners that he hasn't. We are not fooled.)* Unless . . . unless this 'blob of pistachio' is a reference to the Bavarian Charcoal-Cutters' Rebellion of 1756. Is it?

CLOUGH: Yes it is, John Julius. Spot on. Well done.

NORWICH: Only of course, as Hotchkiss proved recently, it wasn't really pistachio that started it; it was actually a rudimentary kind of vegetable marrow.

THOMAS: Was it really? How fascinating!

CLOUGH: Bang on, John Julius, well done. Now then, how about the 13th letter of the alphabet?

THOMAS: That's 'M'.

CLOUGH: Yes it is, Irene. Well done. Well done.

NORWICH: Is this a reference to Savonarola?

CLOUGH: Absolutely, John Julius. Savonarola it is.

NORWICH: Shortly before the Great Recant of 1541, he called for a large dish of scrambled eggs which were coded on the prison menu as 'M' because of the Neapolitan slang for eggs, which was 'uova'.

CLOUGH: Quite right. Quite right.

THOMAS: But 'uova' doesn't begin with an 'M'.

NORWICH: No, the prison chef had a speech impediment.

CLOUGH: He certainly did. That's just what he had. A speech impediment. Well done. And the strong wind in the Balearics?

NORWICH: Surely this is Bismarck.

CLOUGH: Yes it is.

THOMAS: The treaty of 1891 and the so-called War of the Billiard Balls.

CLOUGH: That's it. Absolutely right. So, put them all together and what kind of trio do you get?

NORWICH: Bavaria . . . eggs . . . Bismarck . . . this isn't a Polish delicatessen, is it?

CLOUGH: No it isn't.

THOMAS: *(hesitant)* Could it be the 1969 Young Persons Offenders Act, then?

CLOUGH: Yes that's it, Irene. Well done, the 1969 Act it is. Well done. Quite right. Well, you sailed through that with no difficulty at all; but I think I'm only going to give you 1½ points. Well done.

You see what I mean. Listening to stuff like that fills me with a sense of wonder and awe unmatched since my first sight of a National Westminster Cash Dispenser (I was easily impressed in those days). In fact, although Irene and John Julius do sterling work, the programme is even more frightening when they go Round Europe. When they do that, the challengers are naturally foreign. The point is that they are almost always incredibly aristocratic and high-born. For instance one will be a Crown Prince and Director-General of the World Health Organisation, another will be a Baron and owner of a piece of land like, perhaps, Normandy. Worse still, they always speak English more impeccably than most Englishmen and display an amazingly intricate knowledge of the minutiae of our history. I remember a mixed doubles from Germany once, that went a bit like this:

CLOUGH: Well now, we come to you, Alberich von Tirpitz and Bettina Fechtwengler. So here we go with your question. How much would you pay to see a twisted version of Jeremy the home of glue, some nasty knickers, and Pope Gregory's washing-up brush?
TIRPITZ: This is not exactly one piece of cake (*laughter from all*).
CLOUGH: No it isn't, Alberich. Well done.
TIRPITZ: Is there something in the answer that will 'buck' me up?
CLOUGH: Spot on. Ha! ha! ha!
TIRPITZ: This is your English furniture industry in Buckinghamshire, isn't it?
CLOUGH: Yes it is. But take us a bit further — to Jeremy.
FECHTWENGLER: Shall I take you to High Wycombe — and so Jeremy is Jeremy Wickham: the seventeenth-century wig-maker who stole a bucket of blue paint and was deported to Hamburg where he became kappelmeister to Burgher Grigor Hoffmansthal.
CLOUGH: Er . . . well, not really, no, Bettina. I'm sorry — it wasn't blue paint, it was more a greeny colour. But not bad. Well done. Now, the nasty knickers?
TIRPITZ: This must be Fyodor Dostoevsky and the so-called Nevsky letters about the 1841 Gargling Contest in Nishky-Novgorod.
CLOUGH: Ah — I see what made you think that, but you're a shade wide of the mark, Alberich. Think more of 'nasty'.
TIRPITZ: Nasty knickers . . . not Dostoevsky . . . no gargling . . . ah,

this is Harold Wilson.

CLOUGH: Bang on. That's it.

TIRPITZ: And the Rumford Underwear clause of the 1959 Personal Garments (Soiled) Act.

CLOUGH: Home and dry, Alberich. Well done. Just for completeness' sake, can you tell me who was the Defence Minister of Uruguay at the time?

TIRPITZ: Juan Ginsberg.

CLOUGH: The very man. Now then — Pope Gregory's washing-up brush.

FECHTWENGLER: Might one say that this is, so to speak, a joke?

CLOUGH: Well . . . yes . . . in a way it is.

FECHTWENGLER: Then it is the Franco-Hungarian Levantine expedition of 1843. It was led by Admiral Beatty who claimed, according to Snetterton and Westlake, that he would clean up the Catholic insurgents like 'a broom-handle up a Pope's nose'. Or words to that effect.

CLOUGH: That's it. Spot on. Well done.

TIRPITZ: So a twisted version of . . . Wilson . . . kappelmeister . . . and Beatty. Aha, this is the dancing trio Wilson, Kepple and Betty, and so . . . the answer is I would pay nothing to see them, because I don't like them.

CLOUGH: That's it, Alberich. And neither would I. Well done. Spot on. Three marks. Well done.

I suppose there are alternative explanations for this kind of highbrow horseplay. It's possible that they're making it all up. Or that they are all completely insane and locked into a complicated *folie-à-trois*. I shall have to check with the Bavarian Charcoal-Cutters when I next see them.

Lines Written
on my Father's Knee

Today is my father's birthday. I won't say how old he is since he has the body of a man ten years younger (though no one knows whose it is). I suppose that my father's birthday is really nothing more than a tiny point in the vast continuum of time-space, hardly different from a myriad of other tiny points, but, however insignificant, it has started me thinking. Although I am a doctor during the day, in its spare time my soul becomes that of the writer and artist. And so, on this special day, in deep reverie, my thoughts turn to my father and to the eternal thoughts that his existence raises. Fatherhood. The gift of life. Nature and nurture. The eternal cycle. The immortality of our reproductive cells. The mysteries of futurity. Other authors writing about their fathers. Thousands of books and plays written by blokes exploiting the memories of their old men. Damn it all, everyone's had a go except me — there was John Mortimer (with his *A Voyage Around My Father*), Turgenev, Arnold Wesker, Philip Roth, Mordecai Richler, Mozart, even Jesus. Most of them seem to make it look so easy. They just take a quick look at their daddies, have a brief ponder and then dash off down to the printers with a few thousand words, an opera or a play. So why shouldn't I do the same? After all, my dad is nicer than Mr Mortimer Sr. was, speaks better English than Turgenev's pop and is funnier than Wesker's, although not quite as omnipotent as Jesus's. So — speak memory.

(This next bit is not simply a piece about my dad: it is Literature. You may notice the difference. On the other hand, you may not. It's up to you, but I did want to warn you.) What is the first remembrance culled from those golden days of my childhood? As a boy I saw my father as predominantly a man of contrasts and of curious contradictions. *(See?)* A strong man, obstinate on occasions, firm and unyielding over what he

regarded as fundamental issues, and yet, for all his apparent rigidity and unvarying consistency, a man bespeckled with humour, with inconsistency and a baffling array of idiosyncrasies. Most of them physical.

I think that what made the deepest impression was the way my dad looked after his body. He indulged in an enthusiastic form of healthy cleanliness that grown men usually reserve for their cars and Sundays. In fact if he could have had his body undersealed, rust-proofed and hot-waxed, I'm sure he would have done it. Without preening himself or behaving narcissistically he just kept himself well groomed and highly polished — like a racehorse. This meant that he was under constant threat from a grimy and hostile environment, and the greatest threat of all to his shining-mind-in-a-shining-body came from our solid-fuel central-heating system, which worked (if it ever did) on anthracite, which is a particularly genteel teaspoon-sized variety of coal. Somehow our boiler developed a strange mechanical form of diarrhoea and began to produce from relatively tiny amounts of anthracite, enormous quantities of a grey razor-sharp ash called clinker. Within a few months, we began to accumulate the makings of a do-it-yourself slag-heap.

Now my father was brought up in the East End of London on the principle that nothing should ever go to waste, but even he was a bit stuck when it came to disposing of the hundreds of tons of clinker that we were producing. He had solved almost every other waste problem in our house. He converted the ends of old soap-cakes into new soap-cakes, he knew what to do with old tea-leaves and fresh cigar-ash, he could sort and burn anything up to seven hundredweight of domestic refuse and turn the residue into either compost or industrial-grade bauxite, and he was half way to patenting a method of turning old razor-blades into yoghourt. But the clinker beat him. Apparently, clinker is one of those rare substances that cannot be converted into anything else under any circumstances. In fact, organic chemists tell me that ultimately every other compound in the whole world can be reduced to clinker (and probably will be unless the Americans get their Defence Department computer seen to pretty swiftly).

Anyway after years of worrying about the clinker problem, dad finally hit upon the old detective-story line about the way to hide a book is to put it in a library, and the way to hide a tree is to put it in a forest. I think at first he took the principle a bit literally and toyed with the idea of dumping the clinker in the library by releasing handfuls of it through a hole in his trouser pocket, but eventually decided to carry out the principle of hiding it in plain sight and began to lay out our clinker-mountain as a path round the garden. Over the next few months he produced a brownish-grey path that was not only totally repulsive to the eye (particularly if bits of it got in it), but also highly lethal in that it cut the children's feet to pieces and threatened to start a local epidemic of tetanus (see *Rule One, Drop One*). However, all this was as nothing compared to the effect it had on dad's cleanliness.

Every Saturday he would put on his Chairman Mao boiler suit (how the Chairman would have approved of such a senior executive getting not only his hands dirty but every square inch of skin as well) and would then clinker out the boiler and continue his destruction of our garden's perimeter. He emerged from these labours looking like a Victorian lithograph of the day they finished the Blackwall Tunnel. He would then retire to the bathroom and go through his evangelical routine of shower, shave, shoeshine and shampoo and emerge shining, as he put it, 'like a sixpence up a sweep's arse'. But he was so proud of his newly regained cleanliness that he was very loathe to get dressed, and would spend the rest of Saturday morning in his exceptionally tatty and ragged towelling dressing-gown, showing off his health and godliness.

Unfortunately that was not all he showed off. One of my most vivid memories is of a Saturday when I was about six years old and a lady publisher came round to my mother, who was out. Dad entertained the lady while we kids sat on the carpet being a nuisance. Looking up, I realised that while dad was sitting there sipping his medium-dry sherry and making polite chit-chat, the lower part of his tattered dressing-gown had fallen open and he was quietly flashing his entire cluster at the lady publisher, who was becoming rapidly hypnotised. I was so imbued by dad's attitude to the body beautiful that it didn't occur to me that the sight of my father's bits and pieces was something out of place in a living room, so I didn't say anything about it. Or rather, them. For five minutes or so the publisher sat there mesmerised, making awkward conversation about almost everything else in the room, until mum arrived and took in the situation at a glance.

I have always admired my mother for her poise and social tact in a variety of situations, but for the diplomacy she employed at that moment she should have got a CBE or an ambassadorship. Muttering something about fixing the flowers on the mantlepiece, she walked past dad's chair and without apparently moving her lips said, 'I see that the orchids have come out.' For one surreal moment, before we realised who had spoken, it appeared to us kids that our parents were engaged in some bizarre ventriloquist act, in which my father's appendages were taking the place of the dummy. An instant later dad twigged that we didn't have orchids anywhere in the house or garden, and as the light dawned he quickly (as the RAF say) retracted his undercarriage, and suddenly everyone was looking out of the window and saying how nice the garden looked and wondering where the orchids were and how they were doing.

I suppose it was dad's innocent pride in being so fit and clean that stopped that incident from scarring my young psyche and stunting my subsequent development (if any). That kind of pride did, though, often annoy people. He used to play squash and badminton and, just like people who sit in fast shiny cars and enjoy revving them up at traffic lights, so he would leap around and make self-encouraging noises on the court when he wasn't actually playing a shot. His opponents got very irritated with him jumping up and down on the spot, shouting *hup-hup-hup-ha-hey-hup-hoi-hoi-hup* etcetera. For his part, he probably thought he was being helpful and a good sport. His opponents probably thought he was auditioning for 'Fiddler On The Roof'.

His care of his body was focussed internally with almost the same intensity as externally. He had a minor fixation on the subject of health and diet, and he still believes, to this day, that most minor ailments, including twisted ankle, concussion and heart attacks, can be cured by eating steak three times a day. In his younger days, he was a maniac for the natural laxative action of compôte of fruits and would soldier his way through two bowls of stewed prunes and pears every morning at breakfast. Since his autonomic nervous system was as finely tuned as his muscles, this would invariably produce a bout of crashing flatulence within four minutes. You could set your watch by it (if you could stop your hands shaking). My sister and I got so used to eating our cereal to the accompaniment of this rapid volley of wind, that it was years before we realised that the noise wasn't caused by us pouring milk on our rice crispies. I suppose we should have picked up clues as to what was going on from dad's gleeful cries of 'Goal!', or from one of his two stock phrases: 'That's the trouble with eating tram tickets', and 'Don't tear it, I'll take the whole sheet.'

I don't want to give the impression that dad means nothing more to me than a set of bodily functions. Although there is a very strong tradition among medical writers to adopt the bums-and-bladders school of description, there is a lot more to my father than that. The trouble is that when you try and describe somebody you really quite like, it's difficult to avoid 'Fine Words'. I have spent so many hours at retirement dinners or testimonial evenings, listening to speakers using phrases that not only fail to paper over the cracks and defects of the subject, but actually draw attention to them. For instance, if a speaker says, 'Freddie loves life', he invariably means, 'Freddie is an alcoholic'. And if Freddy 'despite his many commitments never neglects his family', that means that he regularly beats up his wife and children when he's drunk. And if Freddy 'does not tolerate fools gladly', he is simply a bad-tempered old sod.

So perhaps I can give a clearer and more prosaic idea of my father's approach to the world by explaining his method of driving a car. He has been driving for over forty years, and has never had an accident. He has, however, seen thousands of them and never wondered why. He drives very badly but does so with inifinite care (I strongly suspect that this, along with flatulence, is a trait that I have inherited from him). As a consequence, he is often involved in the kind of situation that the Highway Code calls 'a hazard'. Being totally oblivious to his possible role in creating the hazard, he immediately rolls down his window to hurl abuse at the Other Driver (since he has never been one to tolerate fools gladly). He takes no notice of the Other Driver's age, sex, colour, race, creed or ability, but always uses the same expletive: 'You fat four-eyed Turkish bastard, you couldn't put the Queen Mary up Barking Creek.' The problem is that dad, although he drives fairly fast, speaks fairly slowly, and as a result, the end of the sentence is usually delivered about a quarter of a mile down the road from where the incident took place. Consequently, he often finds himself shouting 'Barking Creek' to a knot of uninvolved passers-by, who immediately start giving him directions to Barking. It is greatly to his credit that he always thanks them most politely, then rolls up the window and curses to himself in Rumanian. *That's* the kind of man my dad is.

The fascinating thing about it all is that I am quite certain that my mental suit is cut from the same cloth. Possibly the act of driving a motor-car is to the personality what developing the film is to photography: it reveals what is already there in black and white. (This is particularly true with my skills at colour photography.) Certainly I know that I am a very careful and not very good driver, and that I have a set of stock curses which I produce, like a squid with its ink-cloud, whenever threatened. In which case, this praise for my father may be nothing more than attempted justification for myself. If that is so, then forgive us both, and allow me this space to wish the dear old dad the happiest of birthdays and many more years of being directed to Barking Creek. It's so much nicer than that other one.

The Sundays Bloody Sundays

Sundays, so the billboards tell us, wouldn't be Sundays without the Sunday newspapers. Just recently, in a daring experiment at a secret address in North London, I and four other researchers (two female, one male and a cat) spent two consecutive Sundays without Sunday newspapers of any description. Our conclusion, arrived at with no small risk to our ourselves and property, and published here for the first time (unless it has already been serialised in a Sunday newspaper), is that without Sunday newspapers, Sunday *is* still Sunday. In fact, more so.

I fully realise that my statement may brand me as a heretic and pervert, and in preparation for the contempt and outrage that my confession may cause, I have changed my name (to Rob Buckman) and have had my appearance altered considerably (I cleaned my teeth). I trust the public to understand my side of the story as I tell it, and will now frankly, sincerely and fearlessly reveal all.

Since time immemorial (i.e. 1969), I used to get the two higher-class Sunday newspapers. I shall not reveal their names but will merely add that while the *Sunday Times* was on strike, I got only one. I regarded those two papers as sources of unimpeachable information, highly-informed aesthetic education and incorruptible moral instruction — like a combination of the Bible and the Yellow Pages. Somehow I felt that once they had landed on my doormat (bruising it beyond repair), they had to be read. Like a subpoena or a summons, they demanded total compliance. I felt that if I did not plod my way through the pound-and-a-half of features and criticism, I would stand condemned. I was afraid that something awful would happen to me — maybe my nose would shrivel up (actually that wouldn't be awful at all, in fact I'd pay quite a lot for it) or I'd develop a squint, or a telltale mark would appear on my forehead branding me forever as

One Who Has Not Read His Sundays, and that, as a consequence, no one would talk to me on Mondays. As it happens no one talks to me on Mondays anyway, and they never have, nor on any other day of the week for that matter, and it would have been a nice change to be able to blame my ostracism on a mark of Judas nestling above my eyebrows.

So, in fear of becoming more of a pariah than I was already, I would force myself to plod through a twenty-thousand word report on the Poznan Macrobiosis Liberationists, who attempted a takeover of a Phalangist swimming pool in Brno but left their guns with their clothes in the cubicle. At the end of reading the article I felt intelligent, well-informed, enlightened and equipped with an in-depth over-view of the Balkans. Ten minutes later I couldn't remember whether the group came from Brno or Borneo, or whether the capital of Czechoslovakia was Reykjavik or Luxembourg. As I went in to work on Monday, I became more and more frightened that my colleagues would realise that my grasp of the Brno crisis was tenuous, not to say absent. The only mercy was that, as I have said before, my colleagues were totally uninterested in my opinion on the Brno crisis since they had heard and ridiculed my previous opinions on the Seychelles crisis, the General Motors panic, the Macclesfield worry, the Kingston by-pass, and the football.

It was just the same with the literary sections. Every week, it seemed to me, I was being asked to re-evaluate completely my assessment of the Bloomsbury set. My problem was that I didn't have any evaluation in the first place to try and re-evaluate, so I was totally unimpressed by the news that, for instance, Lytton Strachey was not after all a shoe-fetishist or in love with his gerbil. I read through pages of stuff about Virginia Woolf and ended up thinking that her husband was the founder of Twentieth Century Fox. (On a point of information that was actually the water-magnate Uffa Fox, and his brother Brer.) The more I read, the more I felt guilty about what I hadn't read before and didn't know now. I worried about not knowing Aubrey Beardsley's hat size ('he was a man of curious contrasts — although his feet were an extraordinary and unusual 9½, his head, surprising you by its brilliant lack of surprise, was an average 6⅞'). I ploughed through a three-page round-up of William Morris and wondered how he managed to do all that painting and stuff and still have time to build those wonderful old cars.

Worse still, I found that my attention had a tendency to wander. I would be half way through an investigation of the forthcoming cadmium glut when my eyes would stray across to the glossy adverts. I would dimly wonder whether the cadmium glut could be averted if everyone in Libya (or was it Liberia?) bought a 'special-offer silk blouse at £6.95 owing to huge bulk purchase try it at no obligation to you the buyer'. Maybe the trouble in the Sudan could be resolved by an airlift of 'morocco-look executive briefcases with combination locks that can't be picked (or even opened by the owner) that have these special features look at the special features including a high-security no-slip extra pocket for your ultra-slim credit-card calculator that not only keeps a running record of your personal bank account and sounds a warning bleep every ten minutes when you're down to your last thousand, but will automatically pop round to your bank and apply for a bridging loan'. Or perhaps (I thought) the Islamic revolution would mellow into gentle reform if they replaced all those prayer-calling muezzins with the Sweetone alarm-clock-radio-cassette-sauna-sun-bed that is guaranteed to tan you while you sleep, play to you while you wake, massage your scalp while you get up, make the tea, lay the breakfast table and nag at you for reading the papers instead of making conversation.

The adverts eventually began to worry me. I became concerned about how I measured up to the other people that read these papers. I didn't seem to need a sit-down tractor to mow the lawn and hoe the orchard. I didn't need a solar-heating plant for my swimming pool, a deep-buttoned four-seater chesterfield or even one of those things that you can hang on the inside of your wardrobe door if you've got more than twenty-three pairs of shoes. I checked the front of the paper to see if I had been sent the Overseas Tax Exile edition by mistake. I began to feel that I was trespassing, that I was an intellectual pretender, laying claim to acres of highbrow upper-class newsprint to which I had no right.

So I cancelled my usual papers and ordered *certain other Sunday newspapers*. These *other* papers were filled with confessions and lurid scandal. I read about randy schoolteachers and sex-starved cinema usherettes who spent most of their waking lives sleeping with each other. I read about a retired bank robber whose pelvic organs had been re-sculpted by an alcoholic plastic surgeon and had never looked back (which is what they had been doing when he had the surgery). I read about an ageing insurance broker whose wife, to judge by the blurry photo, was a right old rutabaga, but still managed to have an affair with a magistrate, the guard on the Inter-City 125 to York (and all the passengers), the staff of the North Thames Water Board, and the three policemen who came to see what all the noise was.

And then I sat back and wondered why these so-called 'popular' papers sold so well. The answer came to me with the simplicity of genius: *they were absolutely fascinating.* As we endocrinologists know, the best thing next to sex, is more sex. And if it isn't yours, then it may as well be somebody else's. Since most people find it difficult to occupy their entire Sunday in sexual gratification of their own devising, they may as well read about some other person's. The thing that I could not understand was why, with all these wonderful and lurid stories so freely available, so many people still bothered with the high-class Sundays and the re-evaluations of the Bloomsbury set &c. If other people's sweaty business under the duvet is so riveting (and as a popular sexual fetish, rivets now rate just below rubber and leather and two points above spam), why does anyone bother about the Pre-Raphaelites or the Post-Impressionists?

I conducted my own survey. I questioned closely one hundred readers of the high-class Sunday newspapers, selected entirely at random from an average cross-section of my cousins (see *My Cousin Rachel*). In particular, I wanted to find out what they had remembered of recent articles in their papers. Of the 96 cousins who had read the re-evaluation of the Bloomsbury set, 54 could only recall the marital problems of Leonard and Virginia Woolf and had the vague idea that Virginia was a lesbian who kept on failing the practical. The other 49 cousins (which makes 103 altogether — my cousins breed very fast) remembered that Lytton Strachey was in love with Virginia Woolf's gerbil (this figure includes six cousins who actually thought that Lytton Strachey was Virginia Woolf's gerbil).

As regards the searing in-depth re-evaluation of the Islamic revolution, 76 cousins could only recall the ancient and horrifying punishment for adultery, and the other 27 were actively engaged in adultery and asked me to call back after tea. I won't bother you with their tawdry memories of the report on the Scott expedition, the sexual undertow of the Transatlantic yacht race, or the obscure and sometimes dangerous perversions said to underpin the Minimum Lending Rate.

The conclusion was inescapable. The only difference between the highbrow and lowbrow newspaper reader was the status of the people whose bedtime shenanigans they read about. It was the same the whole world over: it's the rich what gets the pleasure and everyone else what reads about it. It was then that I cancelled all Sunday papers and tried to rediscover the true and natural meaning of Sunday for myself. By ten o'clock on my first paperless Sunday, I had made many exciting discoveries. I found out my wife's first name, and that we have two children and a cat. I found that the spare room needed re-papering, the bathroom tiles needed re-grouting, the sofa needed re-upholstering, the kitchen needed more shelves and the glazing needed doubling. By the end of the second Sunday I had a renovation programme unmatched since the Augean stables got planning permission for a leisure centre. And *that* is when I suddenly remembered why we have Sunday newspapers, be they either sordid or salubrious: they are a useful and convenient substitute for real life and the intellectual equivalent of hibernation or suspended animation in liquid nitrogen. Nowadays my attitude is clear and straightforward: without the Sunday newspapers, Sundays would, if we are not careful, be Sundays.

Stream of Unconsciousness

One of the more gratifying aspects of minor illness is the mood that overtakes one (i.e. me) in convalescence. A short time ago I developed a fascinating set of assorted symptoms. As a matter of fact it wasn't really too bad at all, but a secretary who overheard me listing the physical manifestations of my condition over the phone to a rheumatologist asked me how, with so many things going wrong, I was still alive and paying National Insurance. As it was, I felt all right apart from being somewhat tender to light pressure over every bony prominence and half of the fleshy ones.

Anyway, I looked sick enough to make most of my family think that I was rather ill, and, being the sort of chap I am, I just gritted my teeth, stiffened my famous upper lip and forced myself to play for all the sympathy I could get. Anything to avoid doing the washing-up. All of which goes to explain why, at Easter-tide, I found myself convalescing in a lovely Provençal villa in the mountains high above Cannes.

I stood on the veranda in the evening as the sun sank over the nearby valley. It was deserted save for the occasional woodman's hut, the only sign of life being a faint wisp of blue wood-smoke curling lazily from the woodman's nostril. As I surveyed the scene I felt a deep calm sweep over me. I was aware of a great stillness within me. I was aware of a dissolving of tension and strife. I was aware of falling sleep. When I gradually became aware of waking up, the last rays of the sun had gone, leaving nothing but an amorphous orange smudge on the horizon, and my sense of joy and tranquility in that moment were heightened by that sound most delightful to all who enjoy the Provençal countryside, the sound of the womenfolk preparing dinner.

I lit a duty-free cigar and hobbled off the balcony into the sweet-smelling garden. What an evening! What a moment! What an opportunity to step outside the minute-to-minute sweat and worry of daily living and to commune with nature and to think Great Thoughts! Yes, I decided, now I would pause, take stock of the moment, and think Great Thoughts. Yes, I would turn my attention to a few pithy problems — my blueprint for an Ideal Society, a rational basis for humanitarianism, an alternative to imprisonment as punishment, a peace plan for the Middle East, and a few other odds and ends that I hadn't quite got round to last week.

As I am always eager to share my insights with my faithful readers, I thought that I would now reproduce for you the stream of philosophic consciousness that emerged from those moments of contemplation.

'Right, here we are. In the dusk, at peace with the world. Just like I always promised myself. So . . . so . . . hmmm . . . so here we are. So . . . what? So what time's supper? Now wait, that's not exactly a philosophical premise, is it? It's not stoic, anyway — Epicurean maybe.

'Start again. Start with Life. Ah yes, Life. Life. Yes, Life. Life and . . . Time. A Time-Life production. I once took out a subscription to *Time* magazine: it was extraordinary — every single three-year-old back-number I had ever read in the dentist's waiting room was absolutely fascinating and jammed full of interesting stuff, but every single up-to-date issue that they sent me in a brown wrapper was as boring as old boots. Funny, that. Life, eh? But then what's so boring about old boots? I've known some fascinating old boots in my time.

'But don't boots get old suddenly? You can be wearing a pair of boots for a few months and think that they look quite smart and then the moment you go into a shoe shop they suddenly look as if they are forty years old and you have done thirty thousand miles in them, most of it on rough terrain while avoiding arrest. Nothing ever looks so shifty and criminal as the things on your feet when you go into a shoe shop. I always get the feeling that the assistant is going to look at my feet, nip round the back of the shop and call Interpol. Yes, it was the shoes that gave the police the first clue to the Frodsham embezzlings. Yes, if it had not been . . . GODDAMMIT this isn't anything like a Great Thought. This is dribble. As usual. Start again.

'Well . . . hmmm . . . well, perhaps I should just elaborate my blueprint for an Ideal Society. Yes. Actually my silly uncle Nat once had an idea for an Ideal Society. My boy, he said to me one Sunday, I think there would be a lot less bloodshed in this world (yes, yes, yes, I said) a lot less war and strife (yes, yes) and a lot less vandalism and destruction (yes, yes) if everyone in the whole world spent three weeks a year in the Canary Islands, they're so *peaceful*.

'Mind you, the daft old twerp had a point there — there might be a real future for a political movement to replace Marxism or Fascism with Packagism-Holidism. A new world organised by Cosimo Tours. Are you kidding? They couldn't even get the two of us plus our luggage from the airport to the wrong hotel. But aha! That maybe exactly the sort of world government we *do* want for our Ideal Society — Cosimo Tours regret to announce that World War Three has been delayed owing to the fact that we can't get more than four soldiers to the same place at any one time. Hmmm. So much for Society. What's for supper? HOLD IT. HOLD IT JUST ONE MINUTE. We are not moving from this idyllic garden until we have had at least one Great Thought or moment of insight. Start again.

'A moment to breathe. How often have I asked, even pleaded, for a moment to breathe? Hundreds of times, at the end of the Friday out-patients, I've promised myself a moment to breathe . . . to attune myself to the music of the spheres, to face myself. Well then. Here it is, so go on — face yourself. On the other hand, why bother? Surely one knows exactly how rotten one is in the first place; if one has any sense at all one will do anything rather than face oneself. Deep down in one's heart one would rather face a rhinoceros with haemorrhoids than face oneself. It would probably be prettier anyway. The only people who can actually face themselves are precisely the kind of people that don't need to. Maybe I could take a moment to breathe and go round and face them. So much more pleasant.

'All right. Just for the hell of it. What am I doing here? What am I doing at this point, here, on the seventh stone from the sun, at a flash of time between the first amoeba and the last neutron bomb: what am I doing? Well . . . I'm . . . I'm . . . what *am* I doing? I'm finishing off my cigar, that's what. Somehow that doesn't sound like a very significant answer. I guess I've just used my moment to breathe as a moment to breathe in. So what of the future? What do I want?

83

Where am I going? I am going . . . I am going to have dinner. Yes, that is what I want and that is where I am going — to dinner.'

So I went in to dinner. On reflection I realised that I hadn't quite got round to solving the humanitarianism question or the problem of the Middle East. Some other time, perhaps. I mean life — it takes some thinking about, doesn't it?

Disasters: The Doctor's Roll

The current concern over the inadequacy of our Civil Defence arrangements for nuclear attack fill me with a sense of *déjà vu*. Actually it's only a *soupçon* of *déjà vu*, but undoubtedly our lack of *savoir-faire* and total absence of *je ne sais quoi* makes whatever Civil Defence structure we have *un complet pâté de fois* (a complete paste of time). If you'll pardon my French. Now it's not my place to discourse on the politics and the economics of the Unthinkable; after all, as you all know, I have enough difficulty trying to think about the Thinkable. But for those of you who haven't been following the story, it appears that our government's plans for the populace in the event of a nuclear attack consist of housing us all in family-size shelters with ten-inch lead-lined concrete walls, built a minimum of five feet below ground and equipped with positive-pressure micro-filtered ventilation systems. The snag is that the government are not going to be able to build all that many of these shelters in the four minutes between the sirens and the blast. That, then, is the Unthinkable. Like the *Titanic* it is a disaster waiting to happen (and did not the designer of that very vessel say 'thith thip is unthinkable'?).

Anyway, when it comes to the Unthinkable, my sense of *déjà vu* arises from my experiences as a casualty officer at St. Nissen's. Now in the main corridor of that casualty department hung a wall-mounted white telephone known as The White Phone. And its sole purpose in life was to ring if ever St. Nissen's became a Designated Centre. For those of you who don't know what a Designated Centre is, if there is a major accident or disaster in which there are more than fifty seriously injured casualties, the ambulance control centre decides to which hospital those casualties are to be sent and that hospital goes on to full alert and becomes a Designated Centre. I understand that ambulance controllers designating a Centre are about as popular as Blind Pew handing out Black Spots. Anyway, The White Phone had hung on the wall since time immemorial. No one knew how old it was, but we guessed from the graffiti on the wall round it ('Pasteur is a berk', 'Lister sucks', 'Pfannenstiel is a pfart' etc.) that it was very old. And it had never rung. As every new casualty officer was shown round the department he was told, 'That's The White Phone and it never rings.' And that was that. A fact of life, a statement of pure induction — the sun will rise tomorrow as it has always done, and The White Phone will not ring tomorrow as it has never done. Until I arrived.

I had been working there for about three weeks and was slicing my way through the third in-grown toe-nail of the afternoon, looking forward to my tea and Swiss roll, when suddenly The White Phone rang. Everybody in the department reacted the same way. They all said: 'ARRRGGHHH! THE WHITE PHONE'S RINGING!' And they tore their clothing and ran to Central Sterile Supplies for sealed packs of sackcloth-and-ashes, and started sacrificing their first-born, and so on, in a most pitiful way. Only Sister behaved appropriately. She went to the bookshelf in her office, got down the *St. Nissen's Manual of Emergency Procedures* and looked up the section called 'What To Do If The White Phone Rings'. Paragraph One of that section said simply: 'Answer it.' So she did. I'm sure I would have done the same, though I might have picked up the phone and tried to make out I was the Polish delicatessen round the corner or that the phone lines had been swept away in a flood, or tried to wriggle out of being Designated some other way. Anyway, Sister was told that there had been an explosion at a West End Store and we were now Designated. In spades.

Once Designated, the first thing you have to do is to clear your casualty department of all its present occupants. At that time we had three people with heart attacks, one with a bleeding ulcer and two patients with kidney stones on the go, so we sent them all up to the lecture theatre on the third floor under the charge of one student nurse. It says a great deal about twentieth-century medicine that the mortality of those evacuees was just the same under the student nurse as in the Intensive Care Unit. She later told us her secret of treating heart attacks — every time she saw horrid abnormal heartbeats appearing on the ECG screen, she turned it off for a few minutes and sang hymns.

Meanwhile with casualty cleared, those of us left downstairs set up our triage team. Triage is the act of dividing incoming casualties into three categories — (1) for immediate surgery, (2) for surgery within hours, (3) walking wounded. It is so named because of its empirical nature (triage-and-errorage) and the team consisted of our consultant, Sister and me. We lined up all the crash-trollies we could find — twenty-six in all — in the ambulance yard and then stood there ready to triage the human deluge as it swept in.

The tension was unbelievable. It was like waiting for the helicopters in M*A*S*H and I found myself crouching down with one hand on my head. I stopped doing that soon because it began to bring on one of my headaches. We stood in the yard trying to look as hardened and cool as we could for a total of fifteen minutes. Then *one* single ambulance sidled into the area without its blue light flashing, and its *two* passengers got out and *walked* up to us. The triage team sprang into action in a flurry of clipboards and gimlet-eyed efficiency. The first victim was a middle-aged lady who had been in the haberdashery department during the explosion and her right wrist had been grazed by a falling display of cotton reels. The other casualty was a lady of similar age who had gone deaf due to impacted wax on the eardrum. The consultant took in these details and then turned to Sister and me and said, in his best Douglas Bader voice: 'Triage category three, I think. Do you agree, Team?' Team did agree; so I took the ladies inside, put a dry dressing on one, syringed out the other's ear, and gave them both tea and Swiss roll. And that was it. That was the sum total of what we had been Designated for — sticking on one bit of gauze and filling an aural syringe. I mean it's not exactly the sort of story the grandchildren are going to cluster round the knee in the long winter evenings and beg to be told again and again, is it?

I admit it might have been different in the event of a nuclear attack. I'm told by ambulance control that if a nuclear bomb lands in the St. Nissen's catchment area, The White Phone will not ring, it will melt. Which will save a lot of worry. But nothing, however silly, is ever in vain. Based on our experience, the hospital secretary re-wrote Paragraph Two of 'What To Do If The White Phone Rings' to read 'Put the kettle on and get the Swiss roll out of the fridge'. And

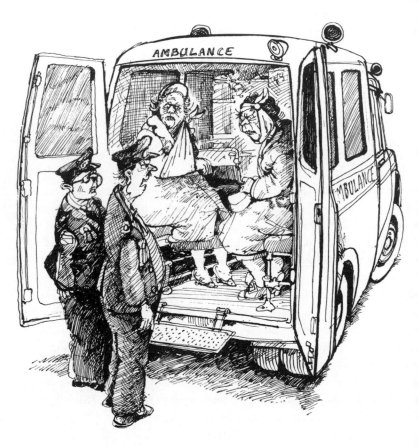

"MAKE UP YOUR MINDS. A BUTTERED SCONE AT THE GENERAL
OR A SWISS ROLL AT ST. NISSANS?"

I didn't do so badly either. On the basis of my experience I was asked to contribute to the government leaflet 'How To Syringe Ears In The Disaster Situation', and was almost invited on to the Panorama special 'Syringing Out the Unsyringable'. As the local Civil Defence chappies always used to say, 'In a disaster, everyone has a roll to play, even if it's Swiss.'

Ibsen: Dramatic Revelations

Here's another extract from my forthcoming slim volume of literary studies and critique, 'More Points From The Moving Finger'.

It is only rarely that a single discovery can radically alter our understanding of an entire era of literary creation and dramatic style. Yet such is the case with the now famous Bletchley letters, a folio of yellowing pages discovered in the basement of a condemned building that had once been a local sub-post office. Unearthed by the foreman of the demolition firm who used the first few sheets for a purpose he has since refused to specify (and about which literary scholars have spent much time debating), it soon became clear that the precious letters were Norwegian in origin and had remained undelivered for eighty years owing to insufficient postage.

Translated with the aid of the British Museum and the Union of Post Office Workers and Allied Onlookers, these letters cast an incredibly new and dazzling light on the plays of the Norwegian dramatist Henrik Ibsen. Written by the ageing Ibsen himself in 1899 to a young and promising Charlie Chaplin, the letters prove beyond a shadow of a doubt that Ibsen's plays were not the major social dramatic tragedies we have always assumed them to be: *they were meant to be comedies.*

Ibsen's first letter concerns what should apparently have been his uproarious domestic farce *The Wild Duck*. It seems that among the sailors of Stavanger the phrase 'wild duck' was slang for an ancient — and rather unreliable — form of contraceptive (*'samlede vildanden til werle ogsaa fagskriften nu cöndöme'*). One can only imagine Ibsen's chuckles as the scene unfolded in which the hero asks the young girl, Hedvig, to get her grandfather to 'shoot the wild duck as an act of self-sacrifice'! The character of that old grandfather, Old Ekdal (itself a joke name roughly equivalent to 'Old Spit' or 'Old Mucus'), was far from being the broken figure of a man unjustly wronged. He was actually intended to be a true music-hall 'silly old man', to be greeted with storms of laughter whenever he talked about 'shooting rabbits in the attic' (a euphemism for 'picking your nose'). Similarly the young girl Hedvig who, throughout the play, slowly goes blind was really a brilliantly sharp political joke about Norway's housing policy of the time. The first night audience greeted the play as a major tragedy on a par with those of Sophocles, and when an enraged and frustrated Ibsen appealed to the theatre management for an out-of-town tour in Stavanger to 'get the real laughs out of it', they all assumed he was drunk.

Hedda Gabler, finished in 1890, was another total wipe-out. Not a giggle from curtain-rise to curtain-fall, he complains to Chaplin. In the final scene of the play, Hedda Gabler retires into a curtained alcove of the drawing room and shoots herself — this was, in fact, an extremely witty comment on the standard of Norwegian interior decorating. It didn't even get a titter. It was greeted, moans Ibsen, with all the raucous hilarity that met the Sermon On The Mount. Even Tesman's next line 'Shot herself in the temple! Think of it!' — an oblique, but rather savage, reference to a leading wallpaper manufacturer in Bergen, was greeted with stony silence. And as for Brack's curtain-line 'One doesn't do that sort of thing!' — an epic parody of a current soft-drinks advertisement — it got, as Ibsen puts it, 'the big zilch, a huge fat zero laughwise'; so different from what he had anticipated (*'hvis du bare kinde pissde hesslves'*).

Ibsen railed in private against the injustice of a world that hailed him as a genius of tragedy, but in public he swallowed his pride, pocketed the royalties and carried on with his secret dream of starting a major new school of Norwegian comedy — the so-called 'fjord fjarces'. In his third series of letters, Ibsen talks about *A Doll's House*. In this play the old doctor, who knows that he is suffering from terminal syphilis, announces that he will notify his impending death by posting a card with a black cross on it through the letterbox. 'Black Cross', we now know, was the name of a highly acclaimed racehorse known for miles around Trondheim (but, unfortunately for Ibsen, unheard of in Oslo) and 'Letterbox' was the nickname of the then Minister of Defence. We can only guess at the exact significance of 'posting a card', but Ibsen writes that his friend Didrik Koht read the script and called that scene a 'fourteen-carat rock-solid thigh-slapping seat-dampener.' He was wrong.

Ibsen tried the same gag again with the young Alving dying of cerebral syphilis in *Ghosts*. His final speech ('Give me the sun . . . the sun &c') was a brilliant pastiche of a contemporary Public Health poster, and Ibsen tells Chaplin that if either (or both) of the plays had succeeded he would then have written a three-play farce-cycle set entirely in a venereology ward.

A great deal of painstaking research has been done on the Bletchley letters by the Clarendon scholar W. H. Smith. With great care and immense patience, Smith has compared the entire output of Ibsen with that of William Shakespeare and in a major coup of literary detective work has proved that almost all of the jokes in Shakespeare's plays that have been hailed as hilarious by generations of scholars, *are not actually funny at all.* He compares the so-called 'fairy-and-fancy' themes of the alleged comedy *A Midsummer Night's Dream* with the time-tested comedy plot of *The Master Builder*, in which a man spends the whole play talking about a building and ends the play by falling off it — a comic seed nurtured to full bloom only fifty years later by Harold Lloyd. No wonder, comments Smith, that Ibsen begs Chaplin to come to Norway to play the lead in a revival of *The Master Builder* — a role that only someone with the renowned acrobatic ability of Chaplin could get the most out of.

Further research recently published by Smith shows that *Peer Gynt* was intended to be a satire on the English House of Lords. The title itself was a very tidy *double entendre:* 'Peer' not only means 'Peter' but can also mean 'Lord' or 'Peer', and 'Gynt' was not only a common surname but also nautical slang for 'haemorrhoid'. It seems that the title role was actually written to be played by a life-sized furry puppet with rolling eyes, but the play ran into financial troubles when one of the backers thought he had developed a rare disease and drowned himself. 'Now *that*,' writes Ibsen, 'is what *I* call a tragedy!' In his final analysis of Ibsen's role as comedian, Smith proves conclusively that a later play *The Cherry Orchard* was actually written by Chekhov.

Whether or not Ibsen will eventually take his place as the true king of Norwegian comedy, no one can tell. It is to be hoped that future generations of playgoers will learn the lesson of the Bletchley letters and that in times to come the death of little Hedvig, the insanity of young Alving, and the 'suicide' of Hedda Gabler will call from the audience the shouts of laughter and the tears of mirth so cruelly denied to Ibsen during his lifetime.

As for the apparently unaccountable solemnity which has greeted the Ibsen plays over the last century or so, perhaps one can only agree with W. H. Smith that 'if a playwright creates a doctor's wife called Mrs Lynge and a chief clerk called simply Krap, and then fills his plays with lines like "this ink is as thick as pudding" and "Gina has had some lessons in re-touching" then surely no one can be expected to take him seriously.' Except the Norwegians, of course.

Hung Over

Hangovers were known to the Ancient Greeks. In fact, in certain parts of North London there are many Ancient Greeks who still get them. And yet, it is well known that it was a Greek sage who first coined the pithy epigram 'nothing in excess'; a piece of sound advice that rings clearly down the ages, and, to this very day, is as soundly ignored as it was then.

The earliest record we have of hangovers comes from the Bacchantes, famous priestesses of the god Bacchus. They would hold regular festivals dedicated to the god, patron saint of non-returnable containers, and it was traditional that, at these gatherings, the most holy of the priestesses were thought to be those who got absolutely plastered and spent the first half of the evening snogging with their bosses behind the filing-cabinets, and the second half alternately dancing and vomiting. It is actually from these 'Bacchanalian' feasts that we get our English word 'wife-swapping'.

In his famous book on the Greek historian Herodotus, the Grable scholar N.J. Trivett mentions that his subject was known to have attended several Bacchanalia and recorded, for all posterity, some of the strange ceremonies and rituals of the priestesses, although he never actually managed to get one back to his place afterwards. Trivett points out that it is in Herodotus' account that we first hear of the custom of dancing all night to the music of stringed instruments (the so-called 'Johann Sebastian Bacchanalia'), and that the word for hangover is first introduced. It is interesting to note that in Greek the word for 'hangover' (which is 2nd declension, feminine — and takes the genitive after 'with' and the accusative the morning after that) also has another meaning. It apparently meant 'a disreputable and immoral fate, worse than death itself'. Thus when Herodotus mentions one particular priestess, Phrygida, suffering from this condition, it is not certain in which context he was using the word. Or, if both, in which order. Since neither was curable and the preamble to each made the other more bearable, it probably doesn't matter.

We next see mention of the hangover in the works of the father of all medicine, Hippocrates. Hippocrates observed the evolution and the natural development of the hangover and, after much pleading from his patients, invented the first cure. He took one cup full of white sand and mixed it with one frond of brown seaweed, stirring the result into one cubit (that's about eight gallons or, after metrification, six gallons) of fresh sea-water in a large earthenware gourd, which he then dropped onto the patient's head in a desperate attempt to induce unconciousness. Of course our modern pharmacological sciences have taken us way beyond these crude beginnings, and most experts in the metabolic disorders would undoubtedly recommend tap-water instead of sea-water.

In terms of the balance of the basic forces of nature, the hangover is actually caused by dehydration, since alcohol is a relatively potent factor in promoting an increased urinary flow. Although it may seem an obvious fact of life, this so-called diuretic effect of alcohol was not discovered until the second half of the 18th century, just before closing time. Even today there are some very strange beliefs about alcohol that have a fervent, albeit minor, following. There is said to be a particularly stupid and in-bred race of men, mostly living in New Jersey, who firmly believe that the cause of the dehydration is the excess of salt in the olives at the bottom of their martinis. It is not possible to talk to these curious men about their beliefs; not if you like your nose the shape it is, anyway.

On a slightly more reassuring note, recent research into the central nervous system has shown that, during the hangover's dehydration phase, the pressure inside the cells of the brain actually falls by a measurable amount. So when a sufferer says he feels as if his brain is shrivelling up and wrinkling like a ten-day-old toy balloon, he is absolutely right. In such circumstances it would be reasonable to warn him not to blow his nose too hard in case he comes undone and goes flying round the room backwards with an obscene noise.

Books on traditional or 'folk' medicine recount a large variety of cures for the hangover. Some people like to go to bed with a large

"DON'T BE SILLY DEAR, HOW CAN HE BLOW HIS BRAINS
OUT WITHOUT A GUN?"

vegetable, a pumpkin or a red cabbage for instance. Others prefer to retire with a lemon sole or similar flat fish under the pillow, or a pair of flannelette panties under the mattress. Still more tend to favour bondage and rubberware, while others just hang around bus-depots whistling at sailors. None of these relieve a hangover, but they all help to pass the time. After all this is the 1980s.

Since the earliest days of the fermented liquors, there has been a belief that a cure for a hangover can be obtained by using 'one hair of the dog that bit you.' Medically speaking, this is as sensible as a man who breaks his arm falling down two hundred steps trying to repair it by falling down the last thirty again. It would seem judicious to suggest to such patients that if they are able to identify correctly the dog that bit them, they should not trifle with stealing one of its hairs but wait until it is looking the other way and hit it on the head with a shovel. This may not relieve the patient's hangover, but it will certainly ventilate any pent-up aggression and is also some protection against rabies.

However, there are other sides to the problem, or, as the old Kent saying has it, 'there is more to a grapefruit than meets the eye'. For, apart from the headache side of things, there is the mouth and stomach side of things, and also the massive marital and domestic upheaval consequent upon all three effects (the so-called 'House of Hangover'). It is generally felt that what is required is something to tickle and stimulate the palate, something to reawaken the taste buds that have been put so swiftly into hibernation. Hence in the smarter London hotels — or at least in those of the smarter London hotels in which your researcher got a glimpse of the cocktail bar before being thrown out — many bartenders serve 'revivers' and 'pick-me-ups'. Generally, there is much use of Angostura bitters, egg yolks, cayenne pepper and, among the more desperate, nitric acid. The idea of stimulation is not, of course, limited to the metropolis, and in certain parts of Cornwall there is still available the legendary 'Piskie High-ball'. This consists of one part orange juice, one part vodka and one part oxtail soup with a live hedgehog swimming in it. It is uncertain whether the palate is meant to be awoken by the swallowing of the whole concoction or whether the patient is simply intended to wait for the hedgehog to develop the hangover.

The sheer number of so-called cures for the hangover obviously attests to their uselessness, and I conclude that the malady is a fact of nature like hardening arteries and ill-fitting waistcoats. From my own point of view, however, I must point out I have never had a hangover because I have been tee-total since June 1968, which is when I had a Pimms and fell over. Even so, realising that I have been treating at length on a subject about which I have minimal knowledge and no personal experience, does not worry me — I am after all a doctor. So, as a doctor, I would suggest that in order to relieve the pain of hangover, you try reading the rest of this book aloud, or chanting it, or singing it, or sucking it, or if all else fails, paying for it. Cheers.

Watch It!

The scene is a television studio set for that most popular of all science programmes 'WATCH IT!'. The set is littered with a variety of odd models and engines relating to different aspects of science and natural history. In the midst of it all is the young science presenter and all-round boffin DEREK BERWICK. His Intelligence and Expertise shine from every pore, but even they are dwarfed by the luminescence of his Enthusiasm and Sincerity. He is a born communicator and seems to be about 27 years old, as he has been for the last eight series.

DEREK: Hello and hi there, and welcome to 'WATCH IT!', the weekly magazine programme that takes a look with closed eyes at the wonderful world of science that surrounds our everyday lives. And tonight we really do want to say WATCH IT, in fact — watch this! (*He holds up an ordinary modern digital watch.*) Now this, as you probably know, is one of the modern generation of digital watches, and it was made possible, of course, by the invention of the silicon chip, a piece of electronic wizardry so small that you can hardly see it. (*He holds up one thumb — there does not appear to be anything on it. Indeed there isn't anything on it since the dummy silicon chip they meant to show was lost by the props department. Nobody — including Derek Berwick — notices.*) Well in the last three years things have certainly moved on and there is now an entirely new generation of digital watches, based on a new and advanced form of micro-silicon chip invented for use on the oil-rigs in the North Sea. And we've got one over here.

He goes over to a table on which is a weird machine about the size and shape of a shoe box. It looks a bit like a miniature old-fashioned stove and has a black bent chimney coming out of the back of it. There is a pair of furnace-type doors at the front, and a piston of the kind seen on old steam-engines driving a large red fly-wheel.

Now this thing (he pats it and burns his hand — but once again does not notice) is called a fast-breeder silicon chip. Like most molten-core nuclear reactors, it works on low-grade uranium ores. What you do is to put the raw uranium in through these doors here, shut the regulator valve here, uncover the core here, and wipe your hands on this towel here. Well, that sounds pretty ordinary, doesn't it? But this little beauty is anything but ordinary — because unlike normal reactors it doesn't produce plutonium as a waste product; it actually produces a much rarer radioactive isotope called Randium-31. When these fast-breeder chips first went into service in the North Sea, the ecology group Friends of the Earth were very worried about the large quantities of Randium-31 being poured into the ocean, until the Government showed that Randium-31, at high concentrations, acted as an aphrodisiac to the threatened blue whales. In fact it turned *them* into faster breeders! *(Laughter.)*

Well, however good a thing this size was for the whales, it obviously *wasn't* going to be much good for powering a wristwatch. But after years of development in — I'm glad to say — British laboratories, a much more compact model has been produced, and here to show it to us is the pioneer of that miniaturisation Dr Ed Case. Ed.

Ed is a spry old bird of sixty. He has a true manic gleam in his eyes and the unsettling habit of skipping while he is talking. On his wrist under his jacket sleeve is a bulge about the size of a large grapefruit and obviously very heavy. He pulls back his sleeve to reveal the new watch which is covered in a mass of tiny buttons, dials, switches and bezels. (Whatever they are.)

ED: Yes, Derek, here's the latest prototype. As you can see the watch is at the moment set in the Time Zone 1 mode, but once I leave any single time zone, I can set a separate time zone *(touches a button)*, store that in memory and start it in Stopwatch mode. Now let's pretend I'm watching a motor-race, say, at Brands Hatch.

DEREK: Yes, Ed, let's say that.

ED: Well, Derek, here I can time Lap 1, store that, and record Lap 2 time. Now I press this button and get average lap time and this tells me the difference between Lap 1 and average lap time, and now I multiply it by Lap 2 time, and I can now store that while, say, I look up and see that I've missed Lap 3. Now I can switch to Time Zone 2, and at a glance I can read out the lapsed time in Time Zone 1 since Lap 2, and there's lapsed time in Zone 2 since Lap 1. This is particularly useful, of course, if I want to pretend that I'm watching the race from America. And if you're watching something very fast, like a downhill ski-race where you can't always see the actual start of the event, you can wait until you see the exact timing on the scoreboard and then fiddle with this dial here to make the right figures appear in this little window here. That way you can get agreement with official timings up to one millionth of a second in up to six time zones.

DEREK: Fantastic.

ED: And that's not all. This display here is the so-called relativity adjustment, which you need if you want to keep exact time when you're travelling at over three-quarters of the speed of light. This dial tells you your height above sea-level, here's the relative humidity (which doubles as a smoke detector in forest fires), and this dial here is a continuous read-out of the *Financial Times* Ordinary Share Index. Here's your distance from the centre of the earth in centimetres, this converts it into inches and this converts it into dollars.

DEREK: And what does this little dial tell you?

ED: That tells you your sock size. And this one here tells you — only to the nearest *tenth* of a second I'm afraid, Derek — that you've forgotten your wife's birthday. And most important of all, this dial, which starts recording when you press the first time zone button, tells you how much time you've wasted fiddling with all the other little dials and buttons.

DEREK: Well now, Ed, that's all very well, but surely what most people will want to know is whether you can use it to, say, time an egg?

ED: A good question, Derek, and the answer is yes. This button here puts the watch into egg-timing mode. (*He presses a button and a tiny hour-glass pops out on a spring.*) But unlike the ordinary digital watch, this new type will not only time the eggs, but will actually cook them as well. (*He presses another button and the watch opens in half, revealing that the middle contains a small saucepan with poacher attachment.*)

DEREK: Well that really is fantastic; but there's one thing I haven't asked you — can you tell me the time right now?

ED: You mean here — in the studio?

DEREK: Yes.

ED: How fast are we supposed to be travelling?

DEREK: Standing still.

ED: Ah. Well, I press the Real Time mode button, and what do you see in that dial there?

DEREK: It looks a bit like a little arrow pointing to the right.

ED: That's just what it is. We follow the arrow which leads me to my *right* wrist and here *(he raises his right sleeve to reveal a normal digital watch on his wrist)* is the real time. Oh, it's stopped; what a shame.

DEREK: Well, never mind, and thank you very much, Ed. *(Applause. Ed blunders out and walks into the scenery.)* Talking of time — a lot of time has passed, and we had better get our skates on, which brings me on to a card sent in by Hannah Gusset, who wants to know when roller-skates were first invented. Well, Hannah, that's a much more difficult question to answer than you might think. Even though man has had the roller-skate — more or less in its present form — for many decades, the real answer is that it was Mother Nature herself who invented it, in the animal kingdom, nearly four million years ago. And it's all to do with this . . . *(He goes over to a large model of a housefly, measuring about ten inches in length.)*

Now this is a model of a housefly — *Musca domestica* — and a very popular model it is even today. As you know, it has six feet, each of which ends in a little suction pad which allows it to attach to flat surfaces. Now in recent times some quite extraordinary fossils have been found in caves at Meiganga, in West Africa. Based on these very unusual fossil traces, scientists have been able to deduce that the earliest predecessor of the housefly — it's great-great-grandfather if you like — was a curious beast known as *Moussaka rolleata*, which we believe was known to the ancient African tribes as the Mbonker fly. Now, as you can see from this reconstruction, the Mbonker fly, instead of suction pads on its feet, had these little wheels, a bit like the castors on your favourite armchair.

So the Mbonker fly, we think, would come in to land and would freewheel like this, *wheeeeeeeeeee*, just like a modern plane. Of course this is a model, about ten inches long, and we know that the actual

Mbonker fly wasn't really this size — it was actually *this* size *(he brings out a model about three feet long)* and weighed about three pounds, which made it much more difficult to swat though much easier to hunt with bow and arrow.

Now having wheels was a great advantage for moving swiftly and noiselessly across perfectly flat surfaces using very little energy. But of course on the African savannah, four million years ago, there weren't any flat surfaces at all, so the Mbonker fly spent most of its time falling over and getting punctures. Which is how it got its name. The next thing that happened was that Man came along and built houses or, rather, huts. And this is a model of a Zulu kraal with its curved almost circular walls. So as the Mbonker fly began travelling up the curved wall of the hut on its little wheels — this happened: it fell off. And it was this action that, we now believe, gave primitive man the idea, two million years ago, of inventing soup. Well, of course, the Mbonker fly became extinct many thousands of years ago, but archaeologists have recently been able to show that, despite it all, the soup is still with us to this day.

Well there are lots of kinds of flies, but the most important thing to remember in the wonderful world of science is that time flies! And our time really has flown tonight. Next week we're going to show our viewer with the most unusual pet — that's Ken Pyne, aged twelve, who has got a pet tape-worm called Wally. So until then — do what you like, but whatever you do, just remember — WATCH IT!

All over the country, viewers are waking with a fright. They hear the magic words 'WATCH IT!' — does this mean that the science programme is about to start? No, it is over. Until next week.

ROGUE MAIL
Saturdays Bloody Saturdays

Dear Doctor Freud,

I'm ever so sorry to be pestering you again, especially as you haven't had time to reply to my last two letters, but I was having a natter with a few of the lads down in Medical Out-Patients and we got to wondering about how you spend your weekends. Well, really I was just telling them how I spend my Saturdays and I just happened to let slip about how I was in correspondence with you about this and that, and so they said why didn't I try and suss out the scene in Vienna. That's the kind of boys that are in Out-Patients — nothing is too much trouble for them provided someone else is doing it.

Anyway, the point is that I do a ward-round on Saturday mornings. Now that may not sound like very thrilling news but it raises an interesting point. You see there are, roughly speaking, two grades of junior doctors. There is the humbler grade — called housemen or senior house officers — whose job it is to live above the shop. The idea is that at any time of day or night there are always doctors 'in the house' available for emergency duties like drinking ward coffee or getting merry and putting plaster-casts on each other. Basically they are regarded as utter riff-raff by everyone in the hospital (except by junior nurses who alone realise that they will mature eventually into crusty, wise and rich consultants) and, as regards official protocol, when all the staff go into the Grand Christmas Dinner the housemen walk in just behind the hospital cat. Above the housemen, there is an ill-defined and uneven layer of people called registrars. I am a registrar and I am even more ill-defined than most. The thing about being a registrar is that, after you have been a doctor for about four years, the authorities reward you for your diligence and integrity (i.e. for staying out of prison) by letting you go home for several of your evenings and most of your weekends. And it is, I believe, precisely because the registrar is legitimately allowed out of the hospital at weekends that he returns to it voluntarily.

One thing is sure: the Saturday round that I do is of greater benefit to me than to my patients. Naturally I look in on all the sick ones, but the housemen are so efficient that the number of times I have had to alter the treatment can be counted on the fingers of one thumb. Yet the mere act of 'looking in' fills one with a sense of some virtue. In fact on an average Saturday morning the hospital absolutely reeks with virtue; it's almost stronger than the perpetual smell of hot deep-fat fried pencil-shavings which fills it at all other times. The visiting registrars (as opposed to the resident housemen) beam with the smug air of Victorian missionaries, and you can tell at a single glance which ones they are. The ones who are 'just popping in' wear very special casual Saturday outfits to show that they are not there by compulsion but by volition. If they wear corduroy trousers during the week, on Saturday they'll wear jeans. If Monday to Friday is a skirt, Saturday is trousers. And vice-versa, even the women. The most extreme Saturday outfit that I ever saw was sported by a consultant in neurology. During the week he looked like a misplaced bank clerk, with a white poplin shirt and thin grey knitted tie. But one Saturday he turned up in a yellow linen jacket, a short-sleeved shirt of the explosive 'Tropicana-comes-to-Brentford-Nylons' type, and a pair of trousers of such dazzling and emetic brilliance as to have made Jack Nicklaus look like an undertaker. Had I worn an outfit like that everyone would have known why I came to the hospital on Saturdays — they wouldn't let me into the synagogue.

But what about the rest of us? Why *do* we keep on popping in on Saturdays. I'm sure there may be immediate short-term reasons — the prospect of escaping chores around the house, dog-walking, baby-minding, sheep-dipping etcetera — but there are deeper considerations, too, and I'm certain you'll agree that it must be something to do with doctors' insecurity.

I have this theory which I'd like to put to you — as they say in the advertising trade, 'let's spray this one over a lamp-post and see if anyone gives it a sniff'. I think that doctors need to see their patients' faces to remind them that they (the doctors) are still necessary. This is a basic delusion common to all doctors, and it persists despite the fact

"IS IT IMPORTANT? YOU KNOW HOW HE
HATES BEING DISTURBED ON SATURDAYS"

that most patients neither want nor need doctors at all and — if they get better — attribute any recovery to the nursing staff. Often correctly. Of course I am being slightly over-emphatic about the healing powers of the nurses, although I do sincerely believe that there are several doctors who would cure more people if they wore black stockings and frilly hats. But even so, there is a strange force compelling us to the hospital on a Saturday. We go because we know that we do not have to, because we have the right *not* to go. Thus we demonstrate our freedom by voluntarily sacrificing part of it. We show our strength by submitting. And it makes us happy — anyone can see that. And surely, if it does the patients no harm (or at least no more harm than we've done them in the previous five days), then jolly good luck to all of us.

Well now, this is where you and the boys of the Vienna School get a chance to titillate your frontal lobes. Last Saturday I was on the wards, strolling along in my regulation Silly Saturday outfit, when I suddenly had a thought (a rare enough event on a weekday, let alone on a Saturday). 'What,' I thought, 'would happen if I *didn't* come in on a Saturday?' The answer that struck me with a cold shock was, of course, that nothing would change in any noticeable way whatever in my absence. It was this that triggered my conclusion that my Saturday visit was basically unnecessary, and so precipitated the course of logical deduction along which we have just plodded, you and I. I went home a dispirited man.

However, worse was to come. When I turned up for work the following Monday (in my *other* trousers) I realised that the conclusion I had reached on Saturday was no less true on Monday. And on Tuesday, Wednesday and the rest of the week. The truth was inescapable: *my whole life was totally unnecessary.*

I began to look around me with newly opened (and slightly dampened) eyes. Like Scrooge on the Third Night, I began to see the possibility of life going on perfectly well without me, if not better. I tried to discuss this new and important view of the world with my houseman, but he was too busy saving lives to listen to his registrar (as usual). I ran to my consultant's office but he was busy reorganising the Phase III hospital rebuilding operation in which all the surgical, gynaecological and paediatric wings would be rebuilt as an annexe of his sinusitis research block, which would itself be an outhouse of the stationery office. I ran to the hospital secretary but he said that he was too busy setting up efficient communication networks between all departments, and making viable liaison links at all levels in a free-flowing multi-lateral information exchange, so he had no time to talk to anyone.

All that day I paced the corridors of the hospital, while patients by the dozen made incredible and miraculous recoveries without my help. For mile upon mile I plodded on, ignored, unwanted and unloved. A deep anguish gripped my throat, a leaden melancholy cramped my tiny registrar's heart, and a clinging black dampness settled upon my stethoscope. My eyelids trembled, my knees quaked and my shoulders shook. And continued shaking. And went on and on shaking, more and more violently and more and more vigorously until my whole body was rocked to and fro in the grip of a rhythmic rocking. I awoke with a start — my wife was shaking me with increasing desperation. It was seven o'clock on a Monday morning. The entire week had not been wasted after all, but now stretched out in front of me — a new week as a valuable and trusted medical registrar. The French Army had entered Toledo. The Inquisition was in the hands of its enemies.

Do you ever get dreams like that? Do let me know, because sometimes I think it's only me,

Kind regards,
ROB BUCKMAN

The Future of Prediction

According to Greek mythology, when Pandora's husband Epimetheus opened the famous Box, he released into the world all the evils, distempers, afflictions and bad vibes that have affected the human race ever since. It was from that moment, said the Ancients, that mankind became the legatee of all such plagues as war, greed, jealousy, haemorrhoids, 5 o'clock shadow and VAT. However, Epimetheus managed to bang the lid back onto the Box just before the very last affliction escaped. It is said that the name of the one affliction that he kept inside was Knowledge of the Future; and that it is because we humans have no knowledge of the future whatsoever and because, despite all our past experience, we have no idea what is going to happen to us, that we are able to carry on our daily lives without despairing, particularly in election year.

It is also said, by the way, that when Pandora came downstairs and found Epimetheus on his knees on the living-room floor banging the lid down on top of little Knowledge of the Future, she asked him what the expletive deleted he thought he was doing. It is rumoured that he replied that he was inventing the pressure cooker. In fact, to this very day, there is a sect of Greek Orthodox priests who firmly believe that all the evils of the world are actually caused by pressure cookers. These very strict men eat all their vegetables unwashed and uncooked, and are recognised by their grey cloaks, black hats, long lunch-breaks and very regular bowel-habits. However, I digress.

The point is that from earliest times man has feared and shunned Knowledge of the Future, regarding it as the ultimate evil. Or at least the penultimate evil now that Donny Osmond has reached puberty. And yet it constantly amazes me how mankind, despite this fear and loathing, is hell-bent on pursuing Knowledge of the Future whenever possible, and is constantly trying to prise the lid off Pandora's pressure cooker with the bread-knife of Prediction. Personally, I think there's far too much predicting going on these days. Now I do realise that the art of prediction has been popular for centuries and will be with us forever (according to latest predictions), but nevertheless I think that we are building up a glut of it: what the EEC would call a prediction mountain. Or rather, bog.

For example, a couple of months ago I saw a Member of Parliament being interviewed on TV outside the House of Commons. Inside the House, we were told, the Prime Minister was due to give a speech in twenty minutes time. Please note: in twenty minutes time. The interviewer (and I have witnesses to back up my version of events) asked the MP what he thought the Prime Minister was about to say. It was unbelievable. We only had to wait twenty minutes and we could have heard for ourselves. If the TV people were that keen to fill in time they could have got the MP to give us a tune on paper-and-comb, or show us his wedding photos, or do a few bird-calls — anything in the whole world (and most MPs will do anything on TV), but, oh no, we couldn't wait, we had to have a prediction.

Now in the early days of man's evolution I can see that a workable knowledge of the future might have been a great aid for survival. I mean if you were a nomadic tribesman eking a precarious living from the savannahs of Mesopotamia, then predicting the next rainy season or drought might be of more than marginal interest. I should imagine that any bright spark who could recognise November coming round again and warn the gang to wrap up warm would be immediately elevated to the rank of seer or prophet, and would be regarded as a demi-god. But can one say the same thing about Robin Day? Actually, talking about Mesopotamia, I recently went on an archeological package-tour there, and one thing struck me with frightening clarity. After nearly a quarter of a million years of cultivating the land with never-ending patient labour and tillage, they still hadn't finished building our hotel. A fact that our travel agents — Fly By Night Ltd. — had failed to predict.

So it seems to me that in the days when life was close to nature, man had an excuse for his constant hankering after prediction; but I do not see any such excuse nowadays. Generally speaking, most events in twentieth-century life occur at such speed and in such random order as to make any attempt at prediction totally valueless. Take for instance the most random situation ever designed since the invention of entropy — a group of commuters waiting for a train to take them home. For the sake of argument, let us assume that there are two branch lines and that one train can only go up one of them (thus disappointing all the people who want to go up the other). Now you would think, wouldn't you, that if there are two hundred commuters standing on the platform staring up at the indicator-board to see which of the two branch lines will be favoured first, then the only thing to do is to wait and see what turns up. But man doesn't work like that. (In fact nobody knows for certain exactly how man does work; but since everybody knows that man is on overtime after five o'clock it doesn't matter all that much, providing man doesn't work for too long.) Every single commuter in the crowd is busy trying to predict which train will be first on the indicator-board. None of those commuters is a seer, few are prophets, half live in, say, Amersham, the others in Uxbridge, and yet all of them are responding to the age-old call coming down to them from the Mesopotamian savannahs to have a jolly good old predict.

Now I'm not blaming anyone, I'm just making a statement about human nature; but it does surprise me that the media have missed out on this wonderful source of idle speculation. I'm amazed that they haven't already sent an interviewer down there. No viewer would notice anything unusual about something like this: 'Tell me, you're a commuter, what do you think the next train will be?' 'I think it'll be an Uxbridge train, Robin, I think the Amersham trains have had it all their own way for far too long. It's time for a change.' 'Yes, but of the last three Uxbridge trains, two failed to stop at Ickenham and while the last one stopped at Ruislip, fares went up 23%' 'True, but that was all due to the chaos they inherited at West Harrow.' And so on. Such is the attraction of prediction that a programme of that sort of stuff would knock *Dallas* out of the charts forever.

It is thus obvious that the desire to foresee the future is a primary human drive — like sex or hunger, or parity with engineering workers. However, there has been a marked change in the nature of the predictions we seek. For instance, in the year 1861, the renowned Zadkiel's Almanac predicted the death of the then Prince Consort in

May. The Prince actually died (of typhoid fever) in December, but that was near enough for the punters. They didn't quibble about seven months between friends when it came to the death of Royalty, and the 1862 edition of Zadkiel's Almanac sold 480,000 copies. A fact that the sales manager of Zadkiel's had failed to predict.

Nowadays not only would poor old Zadkiel have to get it right to the nearest day, but people would be hounding him to know whether the Prince was going to pop the Royal socks before or after lunch, and what his last words were likely to be. If the prediction pace hots up any further, we may yet reach the stage of an interviewer beginning an interview with a politician with: 'What would you think my first question is most likely to be?'

Well that is the situation as I see it to date. Prediction is our new plague and as far as I can see there's only one way to stop it: get rid of all your pressure cookers. That should bring the whole thing to a complete halt by 5.30p.m. on Friday, 18th March, 1983. Possibly.

The Sound of Music

Have you ever thought how important music is to you? Stop telling lies now, of course you haven't. Most people don't think about it at all until it's too late and they're on 'Desert Island Discs', and Roy Plomley is sitting there saying how important is music to you; whereupon they suddenly realise that music is even more important than clean underwear, and without a regular supply of both they'd be sucking their shoelaces for solace.

Well, you'll be delighted to hear that scientists have recently been able to measure exactly how important music is to the human brain with an accuracy of seven decimal places. And the answer is: quite a lot. We now know that the brain responds to music in a very basic and primitive fashion, and that this response begins at a very early stage in our development. It starts some considerable time before we are born, often as early as the second Friday in the month before. It was knowledge of this important fact that inspired the work of the famous French obstetrician Le Boyer.

As you may know, Le Boyer pioneered a new technique of obstetrics in which babies are delivered in a dimly lit delivery room to the accompaniment of soft and soothing background music. This is meant to prepare the baby for its future life by giving it the idea that the world is a gentle and wonderful place, though personally I reckon it gives the baby the idea that it is being born in a supermarket during a power cut. Which I suppose is as good a preparation for future life as any. Trendy followers of the Le Boyer school point out that the soft music allows the baby to lose any inherent anxiety and aggression, and I presume that the dim lighting allows the obstetrician to put the clamp on his thumb instead of the umbilical cord.

In fact, using sophisticated electronic recording devices, doctors have been able to monitor babies' reactions inside the womb to different kinds of music. It appears that they like Vivaldi best of all. Now I don't want to be a wet flannel (although no delivery suite is complete without one) but I do wonder just how important those first few hours of life really are. Opponents of the Le Boyer theories have pointed out that Jewish babies are ritually circumcised a few days later — a ceremony that, even if performed in dim lights and with soft music, is certainly not going to give the baby the impression of being in a supermarket during a power cut. (Although I suppose it depends where you do your shopping.) Furthermore, there may well be long-term effects caused by this kind of behavioural manipulation. Recent surveys suggest that the widespread application of the Le Boyer technique to circumcision has now produced an entire genera-tion of accountants that get severe pains in their private parts whenever they hear Vivaldi. And I'm sure we all know someone like that, don't we?

Well, now that we have established that music is of fundamental importance to the brain, perhaps we can go on to examine why that should be so. The answer is all to do with the way the brain is arranged. Basically the brain is divided into bits called lobes. This arrangement has evolved over many millions of years because Mother Nature has found it to be the best layout for aspirin commercials. At the front of the brain, for instance, are the frontal lobes. These are responsible, roughly speaking, for inhibiting aggression and a few other undesirable behavioural traits. Thus the frontal lobes stop us swearing, cheating at cards and spitting in buses, and help us obey the Highway Code and pay our TV license fees. The frontal lobes are congenitally absent in all Frenchmen, apparently.

In a similar way, neurologists have discovered other bits of the brain that are in charge of STD-dialling, pencil-sucking, tax-dodging and industrial relations. Recently however a new bit was discovered deep inside the mid-brain. It is tucked under the rhinencephalon, bordering on the amygdaloid nucleus and half an inch nor-nor-east of the thalamus. It consists of a group of nerve cells that are responsible for our response to music, and has been called by neurophysiologists 'the music centre' because it comes complete with Dolby cassette deck and free headphones. Using highly complicated immunocytochemi-cal autofluorescent preparations, the scientists have indentified a

"SHE SAYS IF IT WASN'T FOR SOFT LIGHTS AND MUSIC SHE WOULDN'T BE HERE IN THE FIRST BLOODY PLACE."

group of specialised cells that respond to the foxtrot and other classical music. There are other specialised cells that respond to opera, the rhumba and most South American rhythms (excluding the cha-cha which is situated in the cerebellum). In another part of the area there are cells secreting a chemical known as 2'4'diphenylhydramino-butyrate-biryani which causes the owner to do the Funky Chicken and the Mashed Potato. In most people this area is now shrunken and atrophied — almost vestigial in fact. (Speaking for myself, as regards the Funky Chicken and even the Frug, until I was nineteen I was certainly a vestigial virgin.)

It is therefore no surprise that music plays such a fundamentally important role in our lives, even when we're not on 'Desert Island Discs'; and it seems obvious that our particular preferences are dictated by the music we heard when we were in the womb, or shortly after our emergence. This makes it doubly disappointing that I am so useless and tasteless when it comes to music; but of one thing I am certain — they must have been playing a Rod Stewart record while they were circumcising me.

Educating Archimedes

How do you get to be memorable? Who were all the extraordinary people whose sayings and aphorisms cram the pages of dictionaries of quotations? Were they supermen? Were they geniuses from whose lips even the most idle chatter fell in pure crystal form, gathering symmetry, brilliance and momentum on the way down? Were they hell! More likely, they spent most of their time being just plain folks — like you and me — trudging around worrying about their water rates and anniversary presents and constipation. But — unlike you and me — they once said something really bright, realised its potential and flogged it like mad. Compare and contrast the average conversationalist who fills an awkward gap at a party with 'I said something *really* memorable last Thursday at Boopies — damned if I can remember what it was.'

Of course memorability does depend, to a certain extent, on who you are and what you do. For instance, if it's dark and I say 'Let there be light!', at best somebody will turn on the light and forget that I ever asked them. If, on the other hand, I had just created the heavens and the earth and all that is in them, and had looked upon my works and had seen that they were good, then people would take a lot more notice of what I said. Or if not, at least my books would sell better than this one.

As a case in point, take Archimedes. As I am sure you will recall, he was the Ancient Greek who invented O-level physics, and who also said, 'Give me a lever long enough and a place to stand and I will move the earth.' Thus anticipating the Ayatollah Khomeini by two and a half thousand years. I think that Archimedes' greatest achievement was to make up a quote so rock solid that it could travel intact down the hundred and fifty generations from the sack of the city of Syracuse to the ink-stained hands of the typesetters of the cheap edition of

Physics Can Be Fun. I am sure that he had to work hard at it. It's not the sort of remark that would survive long if just dropped casually into the conversation over an after-dinner mint and an amphora of coffee. You'll realise what Archimedes was up against when you recall that, during the Watergate affair, President Nixon was recorded as saying to a henchman 'Get on with the plan for the cover-up', and that this was reported for a limited posterity of two months as 'I've got no plan for the cover-up.' Taking that kind of short-term distortion into account, I estimate that the entire recorded history of mankind has all the reliability of a chain gang of myopic lip-readers muttering 'Send three and fourpence, we're going to a dance.'

There is thus no doubt that Archimedes must have bust a gut in order to protect that sentence of his from similar degradation and distortion. He would not have been able to trust even the most reputable contemporary journalists such as Thucydides (author of 'The Athenian Disaster In Sicily') and Herodotus (of Reuter's). Even they would probably have reported it as 'Archimedes To Start New World Movement' or possibly 'Give Me A Long Leave Says Pacifist Archimedes'. In which case he would have gone down as the inventor of the conscientious objector, and the Archimedes Screw would have meant something quite different.

To be certain that history was going to get him right, he must have covered all the angles. He must have spent all his free afternoons hanging around the *agora* (market-place: noun, first declension), making sure that all and sundry heard him say it. 'Hi there! I'm Archimedes — hey, listen, give me a lever long enough . . .' He may even have given concerts. Much as today the young folk flock to Hyde Park to hear punk groups like The Kitchen Units play songs like 'Sod Everything', so the Ancient Greeks must have pressed up against the earthworks of the winterquarters (second declension, feminine) when the word got round that Archimedes was coming on to do the 'lever' number in the second half. He probably saturated all of Syracuse with it. (This was Syracuse in Sicily, by the way. At that time Syracuse, New York, was occupied by wild, half-dressed savages. As it is to this day.) The whole town would have been buzzing with it after a few weeks. Children would be humming it in the streets. It would be scribbled on lavatory walls, carved on pencil-boxes, etched on breast-plates, taught to parrots and tattoed onto slaves.

And so, when the Romans moved in on little Syracuse, bringing with them the benefits of paved roads, colonial government and nouns ending in -um, Archimedes' little sentence survived the death of his city. Through the Dark Ages in Latin and via the East in Persian and then Arabic, through the Renaissance in what the Florentines flattered themselves was Italian, and finally through the cack-handed printers and boss-eyed proof-readers of Caxton Ltd., his saying sailed intact into the O-level syllabus, where it now nestles against other perpetual truths about the squaw on the Potomac, and E equals MCC.

It all makes me wonder if any of my little straight-from-the-cuff witticisms are going to make the grade. I came out with a real beauty last week, but unfortunately my official biographer, O.W. Tools — he's a sort of Boswell to my Sullivan — was on convalescent leave. It was a real cherry of a *bon mot*; my boss said it was terrifically amusing and my secretary said it was solid three-carat gold. A patient of mine had just had a minor operation that had been closed with a new type of absorbable invisible stitch called a subcutaneous dexon suture, and I had been asked to check on it. I came back and said, 'I have seen the suture and it works.' It was almost as good as the time I heard about a building scandal in a small northern town. 'Ah well,' I said, 'you can fool all of Peebles some of the time, and some of Peebles all of the time . . .'

Actually, I'm having a party when I'll be saying those two remarks again. Come along if you're free. Any time until about 1987. Don't worry about a bottle, just bring some indestructable paper and indelible ink. And, of course, a lever long enough and a place to stand.

Rule One, Drop One

I suppose it is a universally applicable law of human behaviour that when anybody starts a new job they become, for a certain period of time, the New Boy. I suppose it is also an invariable rule that the New Boy feels awkward, foolish, clumsy and mawkish (no connection with the firm of solicitors of the same name). The only unique feature about the world of medicine is that the New Boy syndrome is that much more painful and embarrassing, and lasts a little bit longer, the average being between seven and fifteen years. The cause of the New Boy syndrome has been recognised for many years among ornithologists and behavioural animal psychologists, and it is all to do with the pecking order. To put it concisely, the animal that comes lowest in the pecking order, often called the 'runt' of the litter (particularly by the others), is pecked by everybody and doesn't get to peck anyone back. As a result, the runt becomes what we biologists call 'beaten up'. If after a long period of this established order, an even more insignificant animal is introduced to the system, this newcomer becomes the new runt, and the old runt, delighted to have somebody to kick around at last, relieves the many years of pent-up aggression by beating hell out of the new one. This system can be seen in operation among any assembly of gregarious vertebrates — for example, a duck pond, a chicken run, or the American Presidential Elections.

The world of medicine has many runts, some of them old, some new, some borrowed and many blue. The difference between the world of medicine and, say, the average chicken run (apart from the toilet arrangements, that is) is that in medicine the New Boy/Runt system is made worse by the acquisition of skills. An early mentor of mine put it beautifully. 'Most medical practice,' he said, 'is like riding a bicycle: once you can do it, you forget what it's like not to be able to.' He was a great physician, as a matter of fact, and was later awarded a Bensonian professorship by the Royal College for his long and devoted services to bicycle-riding.

Looking back on my own long and varied career in medicine, it often seems to me as if my early life consisted entirely of being the New Boy falling off a bicycle. There appear to have been so many times when I carried out some perfectly simple and straightforward procedure, only to get blasted out of my socks the next day by an irate registrar or consultant. (I speak of the time before I took my higher degrees and became an irate registrar myself.)

It seems to me that, as a junior houseman, I only ever broke one rule — the trouble is, it was always Rule One. For instance, one of the commonest duties a houseman is called on to perform is to relieve a man's distended and obstructed bladder by inserting a thin plastic tube called a catheter. This is a procedure that requires a little skill and a modicum of strength, and it usually engenders a great deal of relief on both sides when it works. The only problem is that there are about two hundred and ninety different kinds of catheter. Some have holes in the tip, others have holes in the side below the tip, others have angled ends, or balloons that can be inflated, some have bobbly bits at the end, others have three tubes running down the middle, others are dyed red, white and blue and play 'Rule Britannia' when they reach the bladder, while still others are motor-driven and come with heated rear-window and digital clock-radio. The point is that if they do the job they are meant to do, then they do the job they are meant to do and that is that.

So I would be called to the ward, I would look at the poor patient and then go and select one of the nine hundred bits of bent plastic in stock from the side-room, insert it into the patient's bladder, receive his thanks (and urine specimen) and go to bed. The next day on the ward-round I would cop the entire wad from the registrar. 'Goddammit, Buckman, why the hell did you use a Beckstein-Toovey gauge 14 catheter? Don't you know Rule One of surgery — always, always, *always* use a Harris's 16 Silastic Double-Lumen Whistle Tip on the median lobe syndromes up to day three post-op.' I suppose it seems very obvious to you now that I mention it, but in those days everyone in the whole hospital seemed to have a different Rule One for me to break.

In theatre my first surgical consultant made a point of teaching me the basis of operative surgery. 'Rule One of safe surgery,' he would say, 'never, never, *never* put a toothed Parker-Carr arterial forceps across the bile duct without first checking for anomalous venous drainage of the pancreas.' And to this day, I never have. Particularly when taking out tonsils. Medicine was no less difficult than surgery. Consultants were always dashing up to me and saying things like 'Rule One of Neurology — always look for Lucknow's sign in any female who presents with tingling of the fingers, double vision, low back pain and ringworm.' The trouble is that consultants like that never told you what Lucknow's sign was, how to test for it or even what to do if it was positive. As a result, I have always said that Lucknow's sign was negative and so far nobody has ever bothered to check.

Obstetrics was no different. I think that the Rule One of Obstetrics was that every women over 35 who had had a previous baby weighing less than six pounds or more than ten, and who now had short sight, furred tongue and night starvation, should immediately be . . . er . . . well, I forget, should immediately be taken from here to a place of execution and there be hanged . . . no that can't be right. Anyway, you get the idea.

I have come to regard the practice of medicine as a minefield of other people's Rule Ones — the harder you try not to tread on one Rule One the more likely you are to tread on another. But how does it happen: what causes us to forget our past ignorance so quickly in order to drop variegated poo from a great height on the New Boy? I think I can cast some light on the psychological processes underlying this phenomenon.

Suppose that you are a junior casualty officer called to see a patient with apparent tetanus (lock-jaw). You check him over as thoroughly as your sense of rising terror will allow, recalling that tetanus was a half-hour lecture in the middle of the Infectious Diseases course and that you were away on that Thursday at the dentist's. Having completed the clinical examination, you next go on to the second phase of standard casualty procedure — that is to say, you go berserk. You rush to the telephone and call up the duty medical registrar, the duty anaesthetist, the Intensive Care Unit, the regional health officer, the State Secretary for Health, the Minister of Defence, and most important of all, the local paper and the hospital head porter.

Then the medical registrar arrives and goes through the patient's pockets and finds an out-patient card for a local psychiatric clinic and a bottle of a certain kind of tranquiliser tablet. He turns to you with *that* smile on his face and says: 'Rule One of medicine, old boy, these tranquilisers can occasionally cause a disturbance of the jaw muscles that looks like lock-jaw but isn't. Never forget — if it looks like tetanus, it might be a phenothiazine dyskinesia.' Of course it might. You shrivel in shame and embarrassment. Your humiliation and degradation will keep your collar itchy and your underwear damp for the rest of your life and — like all nerve-shattering cataclysms — are completely forgotten in a fortnight. Yet you have acquired a sear: like a wound that is only visible when you are suntanned, it causes no difficulty in daily life. And so your newly acquired Rule One doesn't create any bother for you; in fact you don't even realise that it is a sensitive spot until 4.30 a.m. on your third night on duty as medical registrar, when some fool of a goddam casualty officer calls you out of bed to a straightforward phenothiazine dyskinesia muttering some damned nonsense about tetanus.

It is probably a very deep basic human characteristic to regard yesterday's acquisition as if it had been in the family for years. I suppose that in the early years of man's evolution it carried considerable survival value. Perhaps in the dim mists of time, in the Plasticene Era or something, there were two kinds of Neanderthal man. One learnt a new trick — say scratching his neck, or picking his nose, or making the tea — and when he woke up the next day said, 'I wonder if I can still do my new trick? Yes I can! How super! Etcetera.' The other kind of Neanderthal man learnt the new trick, woke up the next morning and dashed around to the Patent Office. It was this second lot of course that later evolved into Cro-Magnon man and developed shorter tails, smaller jaw-bones and Harley Street consulting rooms. The older, self-congratulatory group, over the years, grew longer hair, developed tiny shrivelled-up brains and became actors. It is not yet known at which stage in man's development he learnt how to diagnose tetanus from phenothiazine dyskinesia: in fact reliable reports suggest that some members of mankind have still failed to learn it. Nevertheless, one thing is certain: they that know it have always known it, and have never not known it.

So there it is, a major component of our mental equipment — and one that I think we should guard against at all times because of the corrosive effect it has on those we seek to instruct. In fact I would go so far as to say that there is only one Rule One, and that is that there is no Rule One. No, I take that back. I think there *is* a Rule One that encapsulates all that I have ever learned about the world. It is simply this: always be very cautious if you are following a car driven by a man wearing his hat. Rule Two is: doubly so if it's a cap. For some reason people who don't take their hats off when they drive are always the worst drivers in the world; they never signal, always swerve around the road and generally behave like prune-brained berks. They don't seem to know a damned thing about driving — they don't even know Rule One.

Gray's Anatomy in a Country Churchyard

This is one more piece from my soon-to-be-published miscellany of literary memoirs and memoranda, 'Pick Of The Moving Finger'.

Whenever literary critics sit down to discuss the Romantic Poets of the nineteenth century, they always agree on one thing: the real odd-man-out was undoubtedly that most misunderstood poet of all time, Thomas Gray. There are many reasons why Gray should be considered the misfit among the nineteenth-century romanticists, the first being that he lived and died in the eighteenth century. However, despite the fact that he missed the nineteenth century by nearly thirty years, Gray was quite clearly a man on his own, a special case.

Recent researches have suggested that Gray, in his early years, was subjected to two major influences that have been, to date, completely unrecognised by literary scholars. It is my contention that these two new facts compel us to interpret Gray's works in an entirely new light. In simple terms, the two facts are: firstly that he was Jewish, and secondly that his parents wanted him to be a doctor.

It is by no means easy to get a clear picture of what life was like for the Gray family in the early 1700s, but it now appears that Thomas's parents — Ike and Sadie Gray — were not quite the landed gentry that previous generations of literary students have believed. It rather seems that Ike was actually a towel-attendant at the public baths in Cornhill and that he met Sadie while she was waiting there for somebody. Well anybody, actually. After they were married, Ike invested and lost their entire savings in launching a patent antiseptic ointment for cuts and bruises ('Try Gray's on every graze'). For that reason they were very keen that their young Thomas should not have to follow a mere trade, but should get a solid and secure profession behind him; and thus they enrolled him at the local medical school.

Thomas took to medical school, as he said in a letter to Oliver Goldsmith, 'like water to a duck's back'. He hated it, and resented his parents for forcing him to it, and it was to escape the unbearable strain

125

induced by both his resentment of them and his guilt at resenting their intended kindness that he took refuge in poetry.

Say 'Thomas Gray' to anyone in the English-speaking world during the hours of daylight and they will reply 'The curfew tolls the knell of parting day, the lowing herd winds slowly o'er the lea, the something something something tum-ti-tum, and something something darkness tum-ti me'. And yet few people realise that this much loved and oft-quoted verse was actually a late re-draft of an earlier poem written while he was a medical student. Like most normal sane students of medicine, Gray loathed anatomy. He continually complained to his parents about the rigours of the dissecting room. He detested the sight of the mummifying cadavers and found it impossible to follow the courses of the various arteries and nerves, or even to remember their names. Because he was so unwilling and so slow at his studies, Thomas was often forced to do extra homework which meant taking his unfinished dissection home with him. Rather than reveal his lack of progress to his parents, Gray would dawdle in the local churchyard of his beloved Stoke, walking back and forth between the moss-covered gravestones in the peaceful evening air, clutching a partly-dissected arm or leg. It is not known whether it was this experience that gave him his later love of the popular sport the three-legged race, but it is known that it was on one of these tranquil evenings that he wrote his first ever poem, the *Anatomy In A Country Churchyard*.

In even the first verse it is obvious that Gray is a poet of considerable power and depth:

> The nerve you hold begins to part and fray,
> The ruddy nerve that should be o'er the knee,
> It's meant to reach the foot, or so they say;
> It's all a load of gibberish to me.

This initial quatrain is remarkable, not only for the perfect command of meter that it displays, but also for the intense emotional power that it evokes. Almost instantly, Gray conjures up his deep anger and resentment of the medical school authorities ('or so *they* say') and registers his apostasy. In the second verse he gives his anguish and frustration a more tangible form:

> My scalpel skims along and, just my luck,

It nicks some bit of stuff that's turning black;
The sight and smell just make me want to chuck,
I'd rather be a poet than a quack.

Surely this is Gray the outraged and oppressed, giving full voice
to his deeply felt rejection ('makes me want to chuck') of the system in
which he felt trapped and snared. Even at this tender age he was still
able to increase the power of his protest by use of contrasts. Over the
course of the next ten verses he describes the quiet graves in the
churchyard and speculates on their tenants. He muses over their mode
of death, the bereavement felt by their surviving relatives:

For them no more the blazing hearth shall burn,
Or busy housewife ply her evening care;

He next imagines the ambitions and aspirations of those buried
there, and then in a brilliant return to his theme, he sincerely wishes
that everybody who had ever died could be accommodated under the
gravestones at Stoke and stop hanging around the dissecting room
plaguing him and his fellow-students with their unnameable and
unintelligible bits and pieces. It is said to be a mark of true genius
that a poet can reach the generality through one particular, and if that
is so, then surely this verse of the 'Anatomy' qualifies Gray for that
laurel. It concerns a much-loved old resident of the village:

One morn I missed him neath his 'customed gable
The house that dwelt so near his fav'rite farm,
The next day he was stretched out on my table,
For me to learn th'anatomy of his arm.

Yet not only does the 'Anatomy' give us a crystal-clear picture of
the bucolic tranquility of eighteenth-century Stoke, but it also gives
us a new and valuable insight into the life of the average eighteenth-
century medical student:

Far from the madding crowd's ignoble strife,
Their sober wishes never learn'd to stray;
I'll sell my forceps, tweezers, probe and knife,
And buy myself a Chinese take-away.

Recent research by the Berlin art historian Herbert von
Trusthaus-Forte has shown that Gray's 'madding crowd' was actually
a group of eleven exceptionally rowdy and drunken medical students
led by the then Captain of Football, a student called Dave Madding.

127

" YOU CAN'T FOOL ME, YOU'RE WRITING POETRY AGAIN."

Trusthaus-Forte points out that no one has been able to find out what is meant by 'a Chinese take-away' or even how much it would have cost. There has been some speculation that his student Dave Madding ('Big Dave') was the 'malignant fate' referred to by Gray in his later poem *On the Death of a Favourite Cat*. There is little to be gained by entering that particular controversy at this late stage.

One can imagine the reaction of Gray's parents when they read this poem. Their hopes and ambitions, so long cherished and nurtured for their beloved Thomas, seemed to be crashing down around them. They tried everything to rekindle his interest in anatomy and to push him through his remaining years at medical school. They would introduce him to young ladies with particularly well-developed anatomies, or slip the occasional abdominal organ or nerve-trunk into his breakfast cereal; but to no avail. As a last resort they tried to turn him into a dermatologist (skin specialist) which in those days was only a three-week course of instruction, but when he turned up with his second poem, *Allergy In A Country Churchyard*, they realised that they were on a losing streak and let him become a poet.

In retrospect, of course, it was their relenting and allowing young Thomas to go to poetry college that was their greatest gift to posterity, and it was through his poetry that Gray achieved the fame which his doting parents had hoped he would reach through medicine. Yet their hopes were, in a curious way, realised to a limited extent. In 1858, nearly eighty years after the death of Thomas, a young anatomist called Henry 'No Relation' Gray published the first edition of his medical textbook, known to this day as 'Gray's Anatomy'. By an extraordinary freak of chance, Henry Gray revealed at a pre-publication party that he had originally intended to write the entire book *in verse form*. By an even more curious circumstance it turned out that Henry Gray had never read his namesake's *Elegy In A Country Churchyard*, but had intended to write his renowned textbook entirely in the meter of Longfellow's *Hiawatha*. Modern day critics have calculated that writing even the sections on ligaments alone would have taken Henry Gray nearly four hundred and thirteen years, bringing him almost exactly to the five hundredth anniversary of Thomas Gray's death. As the poet John Dryden put it so succinctly to

Alexander Pope, 'It's a small world, isn't it?' A point that must have occurred on many occasions to both of the Grays.

Containerisation

There is a fascinating figure of speech called 'The Container For The Thing Contained'. For example, when someone says 'the City of Rome welcomed Caesar' or 'Toytown was in uproar' or 'the White House denied it all', what they are doing is using the word that describes The Container (Rome, Toytown, or the White House) when they actually mean The Thing Contained (the people of Rome, Larry the Lamb and other wooden marionettes, or the President of the United States and other wooden marionettes).

Now one of my favourite authors, James Thurber, once wrote a piece about his school teacher who was utterly obsessed with The Container For The Thing Contained (TCFTTC). Thurber apparently spent much of his school life looking for examples of the opposite — the use of The Thing Contained For The Container. Eventually he came up with a scenario in which a husband and wife were having an argument over breakfast, and the wife grabbed a milk bottle and said, 'I'll hit you with the milk'. Thurber was justifiably very proud of this discovery and mentioned it to his teacher in class. Since there was nothing in her textbook about The Thing Contained For The Container, she became highly ventilated about the whole thing and punished the young Thurber by stopping his food parcels or parole, or something similar.

After reading Thurber's essay, I developed a mild obsession with TCFTTC on my own account. As a result of patient research, I have come to a conclusion of earth-shaking importance. The Container For The Thing Contained is not merely a figure of speech, it is actually a basic trait of human behaviour widespread throughout the whole of mankind, even including doctors. I reached this conclusion after I had spent a total of nearly five years in dentists' waiting rooms and in the lavatories of the upper middle class. There I was compelled to read the glossiest of the women's and the fashion magazines, together with the colour supplements of the Sunday newspapers. Gradually I began to see a pattern in what I read: every third page was an advertisement and every second advertisement was for a part-work or collection. Thus the partakers of this glossy middlebrow intellectual pabulum are constantly being exhorted to buy a 47-volume encyclopaedia, or to subscribe to a 92-record set of Elvis Presley or Mario Lanza, or a 112-disc set called 'The History of Jazz', or 'Four Hundred Great Overtures', or 'Your Ninety-three Favourite Symphonies', or 'A Hundred And Twenty Melodies That Haven't Appeared On Any Other Record Set', and so on. There are recipe cards available in weekly instalments that enable you to produce no less than seven thousand different combinations of soup, flan, fondue and canapé, all tidily printed on easy-to-wipe, easy-to-read, easy-to-follow, and hard-to-cancel cards. There are whole sets of books produced in mock cowhide called 'The Pirates' or 'The Cowboys', with new sets on the way such as 'The Astronauts', 'The Plumbers' and 'The Greengrocers'. By means of a simple coupon you can enter into a contract of such cast-iron constitution that it makes Faustus' little agreement with Mephistopheles look like a nod-and-a-wink, and within twenty-eight days you will start receiving the complete works of Dickens (Charles, Monica, Frank or Veronica), Conrad (Joseph or Jess), Hardy (Thomas, Oliver or Kissme), or Lawrence (D.H., T.E., Gertrude or Durrell).

One firm went a bit further and offered two matching bookcases (offer applies U.K. only), one containing the 47-volume encyclopaedia and the other containing a selection of The World's Greatest Books bound for you in luscious gold-tooled fibertex or some similarly sumptuous polyester vinyl derivative. This pair of bookcases (which will grace any home and enhance any decor) is marketed under the title 'The World's Literature' (I am over eighteen).

Now none of this meant anything to me at all until I ventured out of the lavatories of the upper middle class (leaving them as tidy as I found them) and went into their living rooms. There I found myself confronted with the results of these advertisements — rows of white melamine shelves jammed to the brackets with the uniform spines of The World's Literature and The World's Music. The owners would glance over their shoulders at the serried ranks of luscious fibertex and

refer casually to 'the Dickens' or 'the Shaw'. And yet a brief examination of the books concerned would usually reveal that *they had never
been opened;* some had spines so brittle that they cracked on opening,
others had the pages fused together at the top edge by a melted layer of
luscious fibertex, and still others were apparently printed in Chinese.
So what were these people talking about when they referred to their
unopened unread books? They were of course using The Container to
imply The Thing Contained. They had made the mental leap from
handling The Container (as they took the books out of their boxes) to
thinking that they had The Thing Contained at their fingertips. (In
fact if an owner of the pair of bookcases refers to The World's
Literature, I imagine that Thurber would have called that The Container Of The Container For The Thing Contained.)

I am not pleading total innocence of this vice myself. Many times
I have glanced at a series of articles printed in full colour on eight
successive pages For Me To Cut Out And Keep, sent off a cheque for
£3.95 for the plastic ring-binder To Preserve Them Permanently,
placed the articles in the binder and then Forgotten All About Them
Permanently. What I do not know about 'Warfare Through History',
'The Phoenicians — Fathers of Trade', and 'The Byzantine Influence'
would fill almost three plastic ring-binders.

So what drives us to this curious activity? What causes us to
accumulate Containers and fool ourselves that we are the masters of
The Things Contained? Well, the answer comes from experiments
done on what the scientists call 'the decerebrate frog'. To put it
simply, in its natural state, the frog is green and cold-blooded, has
slimy skin and produces children that look like animated bogies.
From that point of view they do not greatly resemble human beings,
apart from those you meet in showbiz. However, if you remove
surgically the top two-thirds of a frog's brain it is still capable of most
of the normal frog-type activities (swimming, jumping, a-
wooing-going &c), but for some reason most biologists think that it
then becomes a better model for human behaviour. I may have
misunderstood them, but I think that's the gist of it. Anyway, if you
present a two-thirds de-brained frog with a source of low-grade
non-selective information (say a mail-order catalogue), then it will
respond to that information under the influence of three primitive

urges: (a) greed, (b) the urge to impress the neighbours, and (c) the urge to collect things in sets (see *Christmas Boxes*). Even more recent research has shown that the primitive drive to pay out £4.25 per month is only just behind hunger and sex in the Primeval Urge Top Ten, and is fifteen places ahead of the urge to help old ladies across the road, and eighty places ahead of the urge to talk to one's wife at breakfast.

It comes as no surprise then, that from the decerebrate frog upwards, animals will continually try to amass Containers. I was talking about this very point in front of the fire at a rather smart cocktail party only last week, when I inadvertently tripped over The Literature and banged my head on The Music. Like Thurber, I found that the Things Contained can often cause precocious little boys a lot of trouble. I might just add that if you have enjoyed reading this piece or any other piece in this book please feel free to Tear Out And Keep Them: a plastic binder is available from the publishers at a nominal charge. I am over eighteen.

My Body Wears a Suit but my Face Wears Jeans

Dear Doctor Freud,

Your name cropped up in the casualty department the other day and I remembered that I hadn't heard from you since my last letter (or actually the two before that), so I thought I would drop you another little note. As a matter of fact, your name came up when I was called down to see a patient who they thought was about to kill himself. I was a bit surprised to find him in the coffee room, shaking and trembling, attempting to smoke cigarettes and drink black coffee at the same time. So I said, just as a light-hearted opening gambit, my goodness, are you trying to kill yourself quickly or slowly by caffeine poisoning? — cheer up, old chap, things aren't as bad as all that. And he said, your patient is in the next cubicle, I am the psychiatric registrar. I said, oops, sorry, but I do see that being a psychiatric registrar must make you feel pretty bad about things, and he said, well I won't tell you exactly what he said, but the gist of it was that he was going to take a written exam in psychiatry the next morning and so he wasn't seriously depressed, he was just suffering from normal anxiety.

So I said, what do you mean by normal anxiety then? (You see I did a half-subject course in Philosophy in my third year and I noticed that most people cannot define the things they are talking about — being a doctor myself, of course, I don't need to.) That set him back a bit, but after thinking for a minute, during which he smoked four cigarettes and sipped a cup of coffee through another two, he said, well lots of people are afraid of flying, right? And I said, right. Well, he said, it can be difficult to define the exact border of a neurosis, but if you were sitting next to someone in the plane who started shouting 'Oh-oh-oh we're all going to die, this thing will never take off, the wings are far too thin and they haven't got enough engines' and so on,

135

what would you call him? And I said, I'd call him a prat. And the psychiatrist said, yes, well I see what you mean, but I can't put that in my exam paper tomorrow, can I? I said, what's the matter, can't you spell it? — and the conversation degenerated into imprecations and expletives such as often occurs when psychiatrists think you're not taking them seriously. Which is most of the time round our place, but I'm sure it's different in Vienna.

Anyway, the upshot of the whole business was that I got to thinking about anxiety and how to cope with it, and I thought you might be interested in my thoughts on the matter. You know, there is a famous black-and-white picture-puzzle they use in psychology lectures which if you look at it one way is a young lady with a feather in her hat, and if you look at it another way it's an old lady with a hooked nose. We we were told that the human brain (and many students of psychology have one of those) is not capable of seeing both versions of the picture at the same time. So you look at it and your mind keeps flipping you over from the old lady to the young one, and back again. Well, I have the same trouble with clothes.

I suppose it's all to do with the way we see ourselves, and the way other people persuade us to see ourselves. Particularly clothes sales-men. When I try on a smart jacket at my tailor's round the corner (a little place called Tesco's) someone will come up and say, my, that certainly fits you well in the front, while they pull it tight at the back. And as I look in the mirror I force my brain to see my reflection as one of the smart young men in the cinema adverts. This would be the equivalent of the young-lady version of the picture-puzzle.

My problems start when I take my jacket out for a trial run at the sort of places where one dresses smartly (i.e. interviews, funerals and Nobel Prize ceremonies). As I look round the crowd I may see my old friend Frank, who used to help me mend my motorbike. Now in my mind, I have always known Frank in his oil-stained jeans and tatty tee-shirt that shows his manly rippling armpits to such advantage. So when I see that today Frank is wearing a three-piece suit, I do not say to myself, aha, there is a smart young chap in a natty suit, I say to myself, there is old Frank who has left his tee-shirt at home. To me, Frank is nothing more than a tee-shirt and jeans, and any attempt to disport himself in a suit and pass himself off as gentry is nothing but an unsuccessful practical joke. And then I think of myself, and the same thing happens. I see that I have been living in a dream world cooked up by intensive subliminal advertising and bad lighting at the tailor's. I suddenly realise that I am just like Frank, and that I have no real right to try and look smart but should accept my station in life, which is basically to be scruffy and look too big for my clothes. So my mind suddenly flips over, like it does to the old lady in the picture-puzzle, and I instantly become ill-at-ease and start dropping my canapés in the champagne cocktail and forget how to eat vol-au-vent without getting the mushroom-filling up my nose.

The thing I want to know is, is this just me, or is it everyone else as well? Do all the people who seem to glide around in smart suits and silk bomber jackets actually *believe* that they are smart and silky, or are they like me thinking of themselves as untidy louts who were designed for porridge-stained cords and knitted ties that have gone all stringy? Do you ever get rid of the feeling that you are just dressing up in grown-up clothes? Does Lord Carrington ever think, oh my gosh, here I am at this international summit conference and I bet that Mr Brezhnev is really thinking of me as a man who normally wears a comfy cardigan and gardening trousers.

This might just be a neurosis that has not yet been described properly. I really would be very grateful for your advice, or if possible, any cast-off clothing that you think might be suitable. I enclose my measurements and also a photo of Frank in his suit to give you some idea of what I mean.

Yours sincerely,

ROB BUCKMAN

PS   I don't want to appear pushy, but I would be awfully glad if you could reply to this letter. I didn't mean to mention it at all, but a couple of months ago I said to my publisher that I had written to you, and he asked me whether that meant that you and I were having what he called 'a correspondence'. I was still waiting for your reply so I said, yes, that's just it. And he said, terrific, we'll publish it. It seems that your letters generally do very well, particularly around Christmas when no one knows what to buy for their relatives, especially the ones who are mad. So I signed this contract to submit our correspondence and the honest truth is that I've already spent the advance (mostly on stamps for your letters), and here we are with nothing from you. I'm a bit worried because they do say that this kind of thing can be the basis of a legal action — in fact I now find out that quite a lot of people have got money saying they were in correspondence with you, and the police are so used to carting people off to the nick that they have this group called the Freud Squad who specialise in nicking non-corresponders. It would be such an embarrassment for me to go to prison now (with the double-glazing only half finished) that I would be terrifically glad for any kind of letter from you.

From your correspondent,

R.B.

PPS Perhaps you needn't write a letter but do the introduction to the book. I don't know whether you have ever done an introduction to a book before. Cindy in the typing pool says that she was sure you had done the intro to the new Jerome Robbins, but I think she meant Ernest Hemingway. If you haven't, I thought it might be a good idea if I showed you the kind of thing — if you like it, just sign it and return it to me and this will be enough to keep me out of the jug for a year or so.

As ever,

R.B.

It is very rarely that one encounters a young writer
with a true flair for humour. For such a writer to be,
in addition, medically qualified is, I believe, unique.
And for that person to be successful in both fields
simultaneously is even uniquer. Yet this is the case
with the inimitable Rob Buckman.

Rob, with whom I have been in close correspondence
for many years now, has the uncommon talent of seeing the
absurdities in our daily lives. Like all of us, he suffers
the constant 'slings and arrows' (Shakespeare) of everyday
existence, but, unlike most of us, he has the ability to
set it down on paper and remind us all of our frailties in
an amusing fashion. Known to millions of television
watchers from 'The Pink Medicine Show', which goes down
pretty well even with German sub-titles, he has become an
immensely watchable face and there are very few of us
psychiatrists here in Vienna who have not, at one time or
another, jolly nearly wet ourselves at his comic antics on
the box. And the radio.

I feel particularly honoured to be asked to introduce
this wonderful book as I have/have not been asked to do lots
of introductions in my time. But I think I can truthfully
say without any lie that writing this particular introduction
has been less trouble than any other.

To all those of you who know him already, I say well
here's another helping of that marvellous Buckman laugh-tonic;
and to those of you who haven't come across him before, I say
don't waste another minute but dip in right away. If you don't
bust a gut with laughter, you can sue me.

SIGMUND FRUED (Dr.)